NEW APPROACHES IN SOCIOLOGY
STUDIES IN SOCIAL INEQUALITY, SOCIAL CHANGE, AND SOCIAL JUSTICE

Edited by
Nancy A. Naples
University of Connecticut

T0347093

A ROUTLEDGE SERIES

New Approaches in Sociology
Studies in Social Inequality, Social Change, and Social Justice

Nancy A. Naples, *General Editor*

The Social Organization of Policy
An Institutional Ethnography of
UN Forest Deliberations
Lauren E. Eastwood

The Struggle over Gay, Lesbian, and
Bisexual Rights
Facing Off in Cincinnati
Kimberly B. Dugan

Parenting for the State
An Ethnographic Analysis of
Non-Profit Foster Care
Teresa Toguchi Swartz

Talking Back to Psychiatry
The Psychiatric Consumer/Survivor/
Ex-Patient Movement
Linda J. Morrison

Contextualizing Homelessness
Critical Theory, Homelessness, and
Federal Policy Addressing the Homeless
Ken Kyle

Linking Activism
Ecology, Social Justice, and Education
for Social Change
Morgan Gardner

The Everyday Lives of Sex Workers
in the Netherlands
Katherine Gregory

Striving and Surviving
A Daily Life Analysis of Honduran
Transnational Families
Leah Schmalzbauer

Unequal Partnerships
Beyond the Rhetoric of Philanthropic
Collaboration
Ira Silver

UNEQUAL PARTNERSHIPS
Beyond the Rhetoric of
Philanthropic Collaboration

Ira Silver

Routledge
New York & London

Published in 2006 by
Routledge
Taylor & Francis Group
711 Third Avenue
New York, NY 10017

Published in Great Britain by
Routledge
Taylor & Francis Group
2 Park Square
Milton Park, Abingdon
Oxon OX14 4RN

First issued in paperback 2013

© 2006 by Taylor & Francis Group, LLC
Routledge is an imprint of the Taylor & Francis Group, an informa business

International Standard Book Number-10: 0-415-97446-1 (Hardcover)
International Standard Book Number-13: 978-0-415-97446-2 (Hardcover)
International Standard Book Number-13: 978-0-415-65467-8 (Paperback)
Library of Congress Card Number 2005022787

Library of Congress Cataloging-in-Publication Data

Silver, Ira.
    Unequal partnerships : beyond the rhetoric of philanthropic collaboration / Ira Silver.
        p. cm. -- (New approaches in sociology)
    Includes bibliographical references and index.
    ISBN 0-415-97446-1
    1. Community foundations--Illinois--Chicago. 2. Endowments--Illinois--Chicago. 3. Community organization--Illinois--Chicago. 4. Community development--Illinois--Chicago. I. Title. II. Series.

HV99.C39S55 2006
361.7'09773'11--dc22   2005022787

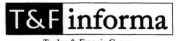

Taylor & Francis Group
is the Academic Division of T&F Informa plc.

Visit the Taylor & Francis Web site at
http://www.taylorandfrancis.com

and the Routledge Web site at
http://www.routledge-ny.com

*This book is dedicated
with all my love to
Nancy, Benjamin, Arielle,
and to my parents,
Irene and Gerald Silver.*

Contents

List of Tables

Acknowledgments

This book, like the events it describes, is a collaborative accomplishment. Many people deserve recognition for helping me along the way. I feel tremendous gratitude toward each and every one of them.

I want to thank those associated with the Chicago Initiative who gave hours upon hours of their time to participate in this study. I am especially appreciative toward Susan Lloyd who, as a fellow researcher extensively involved in Chicago's philanthropic community, single-handedly facilitated my taking on the Chicago Initiative as a research topic. I also want to thank the Aspen Institute's Nonprofit Sector Research Fund for awarding me a two-year fellowship, and in so doing, for acknowledging the importance of philanthropy supporting critical research about its own practices. This money, as well as a grant from the Dispute Resolution Research Center at the Kellogg Graduate School of Management, sped up the data collection process.

Several people deserve recognition for their mentorship during the research and writing of this book. Early on, Michael Burawoy expressed excitement about my intellectual curiosities, continually convincing me that my ideas were worth pursuing. Susan Ostrander steadfastly validated my interests in exploring the contours of philanthropic relationships. Mary-Ellen Boyle helped me to see new ways to develop my ideas. Art Stinchcombe carefully read and commented upon drafts of my work. And finally, I thank Allan Schnaiberg for providing lots of useful feedback while giving me the freedom to pursue the issues I found important. I also feel indebted to Allan for his help in enabling me to navigate the various unforeseen obstacles I encountered along the way.

Many of my peers at Northwestern provided invaluable sources of inspiration and support to me. In particular, I want to thank David Shulman for consistently reminding me of my strengths, and constructively helping me to bring them out. I also feel enormous gratitude toward my close friend Graham Peck for the countless hours of informal conversations we had at all hours of the day and night about sundry topics related to graduate school and becoming a professional academic.

I have been equally blessed to have come into contact with a number of wonderfully supportive people during the years that I have been a professor. At Wellesley College, Susan Silbey breathed inspiration into my sociological pursuits as a scholar and as a teacher in ways that no other mentor had before. She and Peggy Levitt carefully read and offered feedback on earlier versions of this book. Joe Swingle and Pam Bauer have each continuously given me the priceless gift of friendship and have nurtured my conviction that looking at the world sociologically makes life more interesting and meaningful. At Framingham State College, Ben Alberti and Lisa Eck not only helped me through the final stages of writing this book but they have, much more invaluably, been the best colleagues and friends that I could have possibly ever hoped to have found here.

Finally, since writing a book is a task near and dear to the heart, I want to acknowledge those with whom I feel closest. My parents deserve all the praise in the world for showing me by example the value of putting the mind to good work. I treasure the unconditional love they have given in permitting me to chart my own professional path. And, of course, I am continuously grateful to my wife, Nancy, who always gives unabated support, dedication, respect, and love to everything I do.

Section I
Private Philanthropy and Urban Poverty

Chapter One
Preventing Fires while Feeling the Heat

Millions of people carry graphic images in their heads of the riots that ravaged South-Central Los Angeles in the spring of 1992. The dramatic events leading up to this massive outbreak of violence are familiar to many. On Wednesday April 29, a mostly white jury acquitted four white police officers on charges that they had excessively beaten black motorist Rodney King after arresting him for a traffic violation fourteen months earlier. What made the King beating so memorable was that it had been recorded on videotape. George Holliday, a plumbing parts salesman by trade, had been awakened shortly after midnight by police sirens outside his apartment, and proceeded to put his new camcorder to use. In the period between the release of Holliday's amateur videotape and the trial of the four police officers, millions of people—not just in the U.S. but worldwide—had watched replays of the King beating on television.

The three days of racially charged violence that followed the acquittal of the four Los Angeles police officers were the worst riots in this country since the Civil War. There were 16,000 arrests and $785 million in damage to 1,100 buildings due to arson, vandalism, and looting. Moreover, the harm inflicted upon humans was staggering. Fifty-eight people were killed and 2,383 injured (Kirkland 1992; Sterngold 1997).[1]

Los Angeles quickly captured center stage in the national spotlight. Since it was an election year, the media coverage of the violence and the issues it raised concerning race and poverty elevated urban social policy as a leading campaign issue for the incumbent President, George Bush, and his political opponent, Arkansas Governor Bill Clinton (Chicago Initiative 1993a). Consequently, the President did not hesitate to take action, sending millions of dollars in federal emergency relief to Los Angeles within just days of the riots. Moreover, he pledged to a group of local community leaders that Congress would consider endorsing a proposal to systematically address poverty throughout the city (Bush 1992). The President's swift response was, no doubt, built upon an escalating national concern that the crisis Los Angeles was experiencing might possibly "snowball" to other cities.

This concern was perhaps no greater than in Chicago. At a black-tie fundraising dinner a few days after the riots dissipated, the executive director of the Chicago Fund, a well-established foundation, was asked by a friend of his from a local university about what he planned to do to keep the city "cool" during what might otherwise become an exceptionally hot summer if violence erupted. After giving some careful thought to this question, he convened in the ensuing days a diversified group of organizations that subsequently became known as *the Chicago Initiative.*

The central players in this collaboration were foundations and community-based organizations that worked on issues concerning poor youth.[2] Additional participants included religious and labor leaders, heads of city departments, and a host of others concerned about urban poverty. The collaboration's immediate goal was to devise a strategy for maintaining peace on the streets of Chicago during the upcoming summer; Chicago, after all, had had a long, turbulent history of riots (Masotti et al. 1969). A parallel objective of theirs had a longer-term vision: to create a plan for comprehensively rebuilding poor neighborhoods in Chicago, which would address the systemic reasons for poor youth's inclinations toward violence in the first place.

PHILANTHROPIC COLLABORATION IN CHICAGO

The collaboration lasted three years before disbanding in the summer of 1995. A few months later I began a systematic investigation of the Chicago Initiative's day-to-day operation, exploring how closely its everyday practices resembled the embellished rhetoric its sponsors attached to the collaboration; rhetoric about inclusiveness, equality, and democratic participation. To what extent, I asked, did the Chicago Initiative *meaningfully* create partnerships between its sponsors and its grant recipients by redistributing power from the former to the latter?

I became interested in the relationships that the Chicago Initiative fostered between the foundations that sponsored it and the community-based organizations that were in position to receive its grants because these two entities represent such distinctly different strata within the American class structure. The participating foundations were either organizations heavily endowed by affluent benefactors or were the philanthropic arm of major corporations that held millions, if not billions, of dollars in net worth.

Community-based organizations, on the other hand, were typically in desperate need of funds. Consequently, their staffs routinely behaved deferentially when in the presence of foundation program officers. Given that nowadays very few places exist within our society where people engage in meaningful social interactions across class lines (Skocpol 2003), collaboration between foundations and community-based organizations presents particularly fascinating terrain for sociological investigation.

This book documents that amidst their efforts to capture visibility for preventing the fires that ignited in LA from spreading to Chicago, the sponsors of the Chicago Initiative felt heat from the community-based organizations with whom they were collaborating. I analyze the significance of community-based organizations' strategically asserting influence over foundation funding priorities. My discussion develops the idea that philanthropy involves giving and getting by both the grant giver and the grant recipient. Although even within the unique funding context of the Chicago Initiative the two did not exercise equal power to one another, each still had something of value that the other wanted (Ostrander and Schervish 1990).

The fascinating insight that this book uncovers is that it is precisely because collaboration requires sponsors to cede some of their funding power that collaboration uniquely enables foundations to retain control over the kinds of antipoverty programs that community-based organizations receive grants to undertake. In other words, the participation of these organizations in the Chicago Initiative collaboration was, ironically, instrumental to how this collaboration reinforced the power of its sponsors (see Jones 2003). By investigating the distribution of power between the foundations and community-based organizations that collaborated within the Chicago Initiative, this book addresses how negotiating power can become a means toward reproducing it.

Getting the opportunity to undertake this research was the product of good timing and fortuitous circumstances. At the Chicago Initiative's final Steering Committee meeting in July 1995, several attendees expressed interest in finding someone who would investigate which aspects of the collaboration succeeded, which failed, and what lessons the Chicago Initiative might hold in store for future philanthropic collaborations (Chicago Initiative 1995a). A colleague of mine who was at that meeting, Susan Lloyd, mentioned that she knew a doctoral student at Northwestern University who was well suited for this project since he had done prior research on philanthropy. I subsequently began the study with the understanding that people within the Chicago Initiative viewed me as an appropriate person to undertake it since I had not participated in the collaboration and therefore was in a position to provide a non-partisan analysis of it.

My research was both archival—consisting of letters, memos, reports, and correspondences stored at the Chicago Historical Society—as well as based on interviews with sixty of the key figures within the Chicago Initiative. Given my particular interest in relationships between funders and grantees, I made sure to interview an equal number of people from each group (nineteen). Of the remaining twenty-two interviews, six were with leaders of umbrella organizations of funders, three with leaders of umbrella organizations of grantees, four with heads of city agencies, five with Chicago Initiative staff, and five with people who had other organizational affiliations (see Table 1).[3]

Thirty-six of my informants were white, twenty African American, and four Latino. A disproportionate number (17 out of 24) of the people of color were grantees and nearly all of the funders (22 out of 25) were white (see Table 2). For purposes of confidentiality, I do not refer to any of the individuals who participated in the Chicago Initiative by name, and I have changed the names of the organizations that were involved. Appendix A provides an elaborated discussion of my methodology.

Table 1: Organizational Affiliation of Informants

Type of Organization	Number
Funder	19
Grantee	19
Funder Umbrella Organization	6
Grantee Umbrella Organization	3
City Agency	4
Chicago Initiative Staff	5
Other	4
TOTAL:	60

(This material originally appeared in Ira Silver, *Sociological Perspectives* 44(2): 233–52. ©2001 by the Pacific Sociological Association. Reprinted by permission of the University of California Press.)

Table 2: Racial Distribution of Informants

Race	Number	Funder [4]	Grantee [5]	Other [6]
White	36	22	5	9
Black	20	2	15	3
Latino	4	1	2	1
TOTAL:	60	25	22	13

COMPREHENSIVE COMMUNITY INITIATIVES

The events in Chicago that I chronicle in this book were hardly unique. There were more than fifty similar *comprehensive community initiatives* created during the 1980s and 1990s across U.S. cities. Other cities included Atlanta, Cleveland, Baltimore, and not surprisingly given the rioting, Los Angeles.[7] All of these initiatives targeted either a particular poor neighborhood or all of the poor neighborhoods within a stipulated urban area, and aimed to develop a neighborhood revitalization strategy for that area. Although the Chicago Initiative and some of the others no longer exist, many still do.[8]

Comprehensive community initiatives shared two core characteristics in common. First, they did not target poverty in a piecemeal fashion but systematically. Their orienting assumption was that poverty stems from a lack of opportunity caused by a multitude of factors including low income, joblessness, bad schools, crime-ridden neighborhoods, family dysfunction, dilapidated housing, racism, and inadequate health care. Consequently, their aim was not to treat one of these factors but to devise ways of revitalizing the entire social, economic, and familial fabric of poor neighborhoods. In doing so, these initiatives sought to enable the poor to foster relationships with institutions that could provide them with ladders of opportunity for mobility (Fishman and Phillips 1993).

Second, a major goal of these initiatives was to facilitate collaboration between their sponsors and the community-based organizations interested in receiving grant money. Although comprehensive community initiatives also fostered collaborative relationships among other entities as well—namely school boards, city governments, local businesses, and police departments— the defining aspect of these initiatives that I explore in this book was how they aimed to give community-based organizations unprecedented access to foundations' purse strings. Whereas the typical practice in philanthropy is for foundations to decide more-or-less unilaterally how to disperse their grants (Colwell 1993; Nielsen 1985), these initiatives were unique in that they enabled community-based organizations to be centrally involved in both the policy planning and grantmaking processes (Brown and Garg 1997).

This book is the first undertaking of its kind to offer an inside look at the policymaking contexts where the most comprehensive efforts are taking place nowadays to help America's poor. This analysis is of timely significance given how extensively responsibility for mitigating poverty has shifted over the past two decades from the public to the philanthropic sectors. Beginning in the 1980s and continuing steadily through the turn of the century, the federal government divested itself of responsibility for antipoverty reform and placed a mandate on private and local organizations—particularly foundations—to play leading roles in mitigating poverty and other social problems.

Comprehensive community initiatives were emblematic of this transformation in that they were sponsored largely by private philanthropy. While in some cases, like the Chicago Initiative, local city governments were involved, in no cases was there federal sponsorship or participation. The private and local character of foundation-sponsored comprehensive community initiatives reflected, just like the community partnerships created by many universities during this same time period (Boyle and Silver 2005), the broader political climate in which these initiatives came into being. And the fact that policymaking responsibility for the poor has shifted so dramatically in the U.S. is of enormous importance to this book since it provides a pioneering investigation of this arena where so much future antipoverty policy will likely take place.

PHILANTHROPY AND CLASS INTERESTS

My analysis of comprehensive community initiatives supports prior studies establishing links between philanthropy and the class power of elites, while at the same time revealing a more complicated picture of how philanthropy actually contributes toward the social reproduction of the elite. Existing knowledge about the relationship between philanthropic giving and class elites derives from three kinds of empirical findings.

The first is that most giving supports social institutions such as the arts and private education that directly serve elites while providing little benefit to other social strata (Bombardieri and Robinson. 2004; Odendahl 1990; Ostrower 1995). Indeed, less than ten percent of philanthropy goes to those who have less access to the money than the funder (Jencks 1987). As an illustration, Jenkins' (1989) study of foundation funding between 1955 and 1980 reported that only 131 out of a sample of 22,000 foundations gave money to social movement organizations. At its peak in 1977, movement funding comprised just .69 percent of all foundation giving and .24 percent of total philanthropic giving. Of the .69 percent figure, only 1.3 percent supported movements by the poor.

Second, the various social accoutrements of philanthropic giving—such as serving on nonprofit boards, attending charity events, and getting access to exclusive social networks—are instrumental in reinforcing the status of elites. Ostrander's (1984) portrait of upper-class women in Cleveland depicted how the activities of these women—especially their volunteer work on the boards of charitable organizations—maintain class privilege.

Daniels (1987), in studying elite female volunteers in Northern California, also highlighted the invisible work of women in reproducing the upper class. Several other studies similarly view elite philanthropy as a vehicle for strengthening class solidarity (DiMaggio 1982; DiMaggio and Useem 1978; Karl and Katz 1977; Zolberg 1974).

Third, and most pertinent to my analysis of comprehensive community initiatives, the small percentage of total philanthropic giving that goes to disadvantaged populations, such as the poor, typically fosters social changes that are institutionally safe rather than reforms that challenge underlying structures of social inequality (Fisher 1983; Roelofs 2003).[9] Several studies have looked specifically at how funders exercise their power in ways that co-opt the interests of community-based organizations.

For example, McAdam (1982) examined the total external income raised between 1948 and 1970 by five of the organizations involved in the civil rights movement, demonstrating that foundation funding was reactive to movement formation. He argued that funders increased their contributions to these organizations over time as a way to re-direct the goals of the movement away from potentially disruptive tactics and toward mainstream protest. Haines (1984, 1988) used a different set of data about civil rights organizations to give greater precision to McAdam's argument. Haines noted that co-optation enabled the moderate wing of the movement to benefit financially as funders re-directed moneys that they had previously given to organizations that had subsequently radicalized too much for their liking.

Zweigenhaft and Domhoff (1997) explored the motivations that lie behind the tendency for funders—even politically liberal-leaning ones like the sponsors of comprehensive community initiatives—to prefer piecemeal reforms over structural transformations. In their study of funding for "A Better Chance," a program that enrolled thousands of poor African American students in elite boarding schools between 1963 and 1983, the authors argued that the foundations that funded the program were principally concerned about appearing responsive to the plight of ghetto blacks amidst mounting pressures created by urban race riots and the civil rights movement—pressures that might otherwise have challenged foundations' own class interests.

Without a doubt, it is crucial to highlight that foundations allocate grants in ways that reflect their own class interests. After all, their money comes from family fortunes bequeathed by those who are often among the nation's wealthiest individuals, and historically the creators of foundations have been, at least implicitly, interested in demonstrating that the inequities produced by capitalism could be better addressed by private initiative than by large-scale government reforms (Curti and Nash 1965).

Still, a richer picture is needed of the processes by which foundations' class interests translate into a reproduction of these interests and a solidification of their power. Such an account would be particularly useful within a funding context like that created by comprehensive community initiatives, where the outpouring of grants was in many cases ongoing and where grantmaking decisions were made collaboratively between funders and grantees.

We can begin to deepen the analysis by recognizing, firstly, that seeing foundations as simply acting upon underlying class interests fails to take into account potentially important variation among them. Jenkins and Eckert (1986) point out in their study of the array of funders that supported the civil rights movement that community-based organizations' goals were co-opted even though many of the grants came from foundations that had pronounced and longstanding commitments to combat institutionalized racism toward African Americans. Their study underscores that foundations typically have a vocabulary of motives (Mills 1940) that include both the desire to protect class interests and to redress particular social problems. Whether these motives are genuine and sincere or simply staged is a question for empirical research that I do not undertake in this book. Certainly, attention must be given, as my ensuing analysis of the Chicago Initiative does, to the ways that foundations strategically portray images of social concern in an effort to mask their underlying class interests.

Secondly, we must recognize the ways that grantees can be actively involved in influencing funding decisions. Their influence is particularly important to investigate within the collaborative context of comprehensive community initiatives. As I will illustrate throughout the book, even though the sponsors of these initiatives exercised an upper hand over community-based organizations since they had money that these organizations crucially needed, funders' efforts to attach prestige to their claimed concerns about ameliorating urban poverty through these initiatives made them dependent on grantees for legitimation. By virtue of their very interest in being accountable to the organizations they supported, funders implicitly sought their grantees' validation. The irony here is that those grantees that are typically among the most financially dependent on funders (small organizations doing antipoverty work) often have the most extensive power to legitimate funders' identity as socially responsible for redressing what one of the funders I interviewed described as "*the* problem of the metropolis—the overwhelming joblessness in a community that is segregated, discriminated against, and having a terrible time in school."

ELITES, SUBORDINATES, AND RESISTANCE

In illuminating how collaborative funding arrangements enable foundations to co-opt the programming work of community-based organizations, this book addresses more broadly how the social reproduction of elite power occurs through the *interplay* of a system of domination—in this case, funding practices that serve foundations' class interests—and acts of resistance toward that system.

Prior studies of social contexts that widely diverge from the comprehensive community initiatives I investigate in this book offer a template for the analysis I provide and the conclusions I subsequently draw from it. For example, in his ethnographic study of a British school, Willis (1977) illustrated that the lads, a group of non-conformist working-class boys, moved into working-class jobs because they openly resisted the school's official message that conformity and hard work would lead them to middle-class futures. Indeed, it was precisely through their rejection of the school's ideology that the lads reproduced their existing class position. This study substantiated that social reproduction of an elite's ideology—in this case, the school's interest in producing future middle class professionals—occurs because of how subordinates actively make un-coerced decisions affecting their futures.

Jay MacLeod's more recent ethnography (2004) compared the mechanisms of social reproduction for the Hallway Hangers, a group of non-conformist boys similar to the lads, and the Brothers, a different group of working class boys that fully subscribed to their high school's middle class ideology. The fact that MacLeod studied two groups of working-class youth that experienced social reproduction differently supports Willis' argument that social reproduction is not simply determined by elites, but rather occurs through negotiated interaction between dominant and subordinate groups.

The most important work that informs my analysis of comprehensive community initiatives is James Scott's (1985, 1989, 1990) research about how dominant groups maintain their power in the face of disguised forms of resistance. Scott studied different "theaters" of everyday social interaction between dominant and subordinate groups. He construed the *public transcript* as the front-stage interaction between these groups, in which the former set the terms of the relationship while subordinates generously pay deference to them. Although on the front stage subordinate groups must credibly act in accordance with the official story of power projected by dominant groups, back stage lies a *hidden transcript* consisting of subordinate groups' insurgent beliefs, practices, and gestures that collectively exhibit resistance toward this official story.

ORGANIZATION OF THE BOOK

Chapter Two provides a historical context for understanding foundations' interest in comprehensive community initiatives as a strategy of antipoverty reform. In particular, I show how these initiatives, which all unfolded without support from the federal government, reflected the political climate that existed during the period they came into being—the 1980s and 1990s. This was a period characterized by a major transformation in responsibility for social policy from the federal government to private and local organizations.

The next three chapters trace the story of the Chicago Initiative by documenting the events that unfolded from its inception in May 1992 until its closing in August 1995. Although I refer to many of the key events in the Initiative's history, my discussion does not aim to be a definitive historical treatment of the subject. Rather, it provides insight into the sociological importance of comprehensive community initiatives as a whole. So that as my narrative unfolds the reader will have a clear sense of the chronology of the Chicago Initiative, I have listed key dates in Appendix B.

Chapter Three examines the context in which funders framed the 1992 LA riots as a crisis demanding their immediate response, and consequently mobilized the Chicago Initiative in an effort to prevent similar violence from occurring locally. Funders allocated grants to community-based organizations in order to expand opportunities for poor youth while they were out of school for the summer. Funders also set in motion an investigation of ways that the Chicago Initiative might embrace a long-range plan for the revitalization of low-income neighborhoods in the city. I show how sponsors' support for the Chicago Initiative was founded upon an interest in gaining prestige for coming to the aid of the poor amidst a crisis.

Chapter Four explores the reasons that community-based organizations participated in the Chicago Initiative. These organizations faced a dilemma: although they cynically viewed the Initiative as the latest faddish effort by elites to demonstrate sustained concern for the poor, these organizations desperately needed the funds the Initiative made available to them. Some community-based organizations got involved simply to access wider sources of funding while others were inspired by the opportunity the collaboration afforded them to devise a long-range neighborhood revitalization agenda for Chicago that might elicit funders' sustained support.

In Chapter Five, the discussion turns to why many funders sustained a three-year interest in the Chicago Initiative and yet did not embrace the kind of long-range vision that community leaders had for the collaboration. My narrative of the reasons behind the closing of the Initiative in August

1995 reveals key attributes of foundations' grantmaking culture. Understanding this culture helps to explain how funders could be ideologically committed to a particular agenda—in this case, the revitalization of poor urban neighborhoods—but still not fund it.

The final two chapters step back from the day-to-day details of the Chicago Initiative story and analyze the wider implications of this story. Chapter Six considers what this case study reveals about collaboration as a strategy of antipoverty reform. I argue that collaboration produced an insidious context for funders to co-opt the work of community-based organizations, and therefore the collaboration actually served to reproduce the very power disparities between foundations and community-based organizations that it purported to mitigate.

Chapter Seven concludes the book by pointing out that substantial amounts of philanthropy are typically only given when a social problem is able to capture and sustains the media spotlight, as was certainly the case with the Chicago Initiative's response to the 1992 LA riots. I compare the Initiative with the massive worldwide pooling of charitable contributions that followed the devastating Indian Ocean tsunami in December 2004. This comparison reveals how philanthropy plays a central role in the construction of a problem as an issue of top concern. Since news coverage is so influential in framing how people think about the urgency of addressing one problem over another, philanthropic giving that is concentrated toward problems highlighted by the media serves as a secondary "spotlight" for these issues.

Chapter Two

As American as Apple Pie: The Tradition of Private and Local Antipoverty Reform in the U.S.

The historical record documents social concern exhibited toward the plight of the poor dating as far back as the earliest settlers to the New World. Within Colonial America, a tradition emerged whereby relief efforts chiefly took place either privately or through local government action. This was to remain the case well into the 20th century, with the federal government remaining largely on the sidelines when it came to matters concerning the social welfare of America's poor.

And when the federal welfare state did begin to take shape, and consequently grow massively during the 1930s under President Franklin Roosevelt, it did so in large part through the efforts of the many private philanthropic foundations that had come into being a few decades earlier. These endowed organizations indeed were to play important roles in shaping national antipoverty policy. Foundations' influence upon the growth of the welfare state was greatest in the years surrounding the federal government's "war on poverty" during the 1960s. As the welfare state dramatically shrunk during the 1980s and 1990s, foundations began to assume an unprecedented center-stage role in the making of antipoverty reform, most notably through their sponsorship of comprehensive community initiatives.

PRIVATE AND LOCAL: ANTIPOVERTY REFORM IN THE U.S. UNTIL THE EARLY 20TH CENTURY

Beginning with Plymouth in 1642, the colonies of the New World passed a series of "poor laws" over the next several decades. Modeled after the

Elizabethan Poor Law of 1601, the colonial legislation vested administrative responsibility toward the poor within the most local level of government, which in the northern colonies was the town and in the southern colonies the church parish. In both cases, local officials collected taxes that were used to cover the food, clothing, and medical expenses associated with the placement of needy individuals in private homes—a reform measure that became known as "home relief." Private charity also supplemented the aid provided under the poor laws. Up through the early years of the new republic, locally administered public assistance and private charity gradually grew to become twin engines of support for the poor (Trattner 1984).

During the early 19th century, the poor laws came under attack. Whereas until this point evidence of material need alone drove relief efforts, a belief now began to emerge that regarded the able-bodied poor as blameworthy for their impoverished conditions. This view consequently held that public aid only served to keep people poor. On top of this was a growing antagonism toward recipients of public aid who saw home relief as their right, and hence did not express gratitude toward those who provided it to them.

These criticisms of the poor laws spawned efforts to create a new kind of social welfare. In the early 1820s, the New York legislature commissioned Secretary of State J.V.N. Yates to do a survey of public aid throughout the state, and the subsequently produced Yates Report was to become a blueprint for future poverty reform. Counties, as opposed to towns previously, now became the administrators of two kinds of new institutions. Almshouses provided ongoing care for the "worthy" poor (those who were poor because they were unable to work)—a group that included children, the elderly, and the physically handicapped. Workhouses assisted the able-bodied, or "unworthy," poor to acquire the motivation and work ethic they needed to improve their material conditions. Although home relief was not abolished all at once, by the end of the Civil War "institutional relief" had become a common form of social welfare and had become the primary source of assistance to the poor by the turn of the 20th century (Trattner 1984).

During the years that institutional relief gradually replaced home relief as the dominant form of poor support, another kind of private initiative was taking hold. A group of white Protestant professionals created "benevolent societies" through their charitable giving, as a way of improving the moral character of the rising number of poor Catholic immigrants living within urban areas. Two popular beliefs guided the work of these charitable men. First, in a land of plentiful resources and limitless opportunities poverty arose when intemperate individuals failed to exercise sufficient discipline to value hard work over drinking. And second, home relief only served to foster public dependence for these people who were unworthy of such support in the first place. The founders of benevolent societies sought not to provide material relief but to inculcate poor individuals with Protestant values concerning sobriety, industriousness, and the sacrificing of immediate gratification for future reward (Trattner 1984).

Despite the overriding sentiment that had, by the end of the Civil War, grown *against* both the private and public administration of material aid to the poor, in the wake of economic depression these sentiments subsided. During the 1870s approximately three million men lost their jobs and rioting occurred following the failed attempts of the unemployed to secure local and state provisions for public works programs. Amidst these episodes of violence, both private and public sources responded with massive relief efforts that were based upon very little assessment of legitimate need. These efforts included setting up breadlines, soup kitchens, and free lodging houses as well as distributing clothing, coal, food, and cash (Trattner 1984).

Yet, as the economic crisis abated, critical sentiment toward the provision of material relief returned. The re-emergence of this sentiment sped up the shift from home to institutional relief as well as led to calls for private charity to become more scientific. The "charity organization society" movement that subsequently emerged created new administrative bodies to oversee the relief efforts that had become, against their original design, part of the work of the burgeoning number of benevolent societies that now existed across American cities. These new charitable organizations kept detailed records of applicants for aid and referred those that were worthy of assistance to the appropriate relief agency. The key work of charity organization societies was rigorous scientific investigation into the causes of poverty. Volunteer workers—most of whom were well-to-do women who felt a social responsibility toward the needy—made inquiries concerning appeals by poor people for public assistance in order to ensure that relief was made available only to those deemed worthy of support (Paterson 2000; Trattner 1984).

During the 1890s, charity organization societies began to change their view toward the poor. A number of studies were published indicating that structural factors such as unemployment, overwork, low wages, dangerous working conditions, and unsanitary living conditions were a much more likely cause of poverty than individual factors such as shiftlessness, intemperance, and improvidence. These studies fostered a new image of the poor: that they had as much moral virtue as did any other group of people. As a result of this changed imagery, the charitable work of volunteers gradually became professionalized. Since poverty was now seen as a problem that lay outside the individual, the need arose for people with the necessary training and experience to tackle this deep-seated problem (Trattner 1984).

The earliest manifestation of the shift toward professionalized poverty reform was the settlement house movement. Unlike prior relief efforts initiated by either local governments or private charities, the goal of settlement houses was to promote change by enabling poor people to attain greater access to economic and social opportunity. Whereas previous reformers made distinctions between the "worthy" and "unworthy" poor (tending to aid only the former), settlement house workers focused on the structural forces that similarly affected all impoverished people. These workers neither disparaged nor looked down upon the poor, but rather encouraged those poor people who were recent immigrants to the U.S. to retain pride in their Old World heritage (Paterson 2000; Trattner 1984).

Settlement house workers tended to be single college-educated women in their twenties who were from well-to-do families and who were religiously motivated to serve the poor. These women had a vision for bridging class divisions within America's cities, believing that meaningful social change could only occur if they themselves lived among the poor and learned first-hand about the kinds of conditions they faced. Settlement houses initially sought to establish rapport with the local community by creating kindergartens, nurseries, and daycare centers so that working mothers had a safe place to leave their children and children had spaces in which to play. Settlement houses subsequently added libraries, gymnasiums, employment bureaus, and various other services.

Although these services did not address the deep-seated causes of poverty, settlement houses still achieved two noteworthy results. First, they exhibited a level of racial tolerance that was unprecedented compared to prior poverty relief efforts, which generally ignored the problems of blacks. Second, settlement houses created an atmosphere of cooperation between reformers and residents that had not previously existed within poor neighborhoods (Trattner 1984).

As the settlement house movement spread (there were four hundred settlement houses in operation by 1910), they began to merge with charity organization societies to create what became the modern social work agency. The institutionalization of social work gradually caused the work of settlement house residents to seem old-fashioned and the idea of reformers living amidst the poor to go into disfavor. With the new cadre of professional social workers often more interested in developing relationships with their colleagues than with the populations they served, the links that settlement houses had forged between reformers and poor residents gradually began to disintegrate (Trattner 1984).

The movement to professionalize poverty reform, which first emerged through the work of charity organization societies and became institutionalized as clinical social work grew to prominence, also manifested itself in the emergence of private foundations. During the late nineteenth and early twentieth centuries, a group of prominent businessmen created this new organizational form with the fortunes they had amassed during the years of industrial growth following the Civil War. These men approached social reform with the same kind of scientific rigor that they saw as critical to their successes in business. They were interested in understanding the causes of social problems, and sought to use this knowledge to attack problems in ways that prior charitable relief work had not. Herein lay a critical distinction they made between *charity* and *philanthropy*. Whereas charity was meant to alleviate the effects of social problems, these men endowed foundations in order to advance a philanthropic agenda: scientifically rooting out these problems altogether (Karl and Katz 1981; Nielsen 1985; Smith 1999).

During the early twentieth century, private foundations—most notably the Rockefeller, Carnegie, and Sage Foundations—became incorporated as not-for-profit, non-governmental organizations chartered to advance broadly defined goals in support of the public good. These foundations were a cornerstone of the wider movement, reflected by the prior emergence of settlement houses and professional social work, to advance *private* solutions to poverty and other social problems. This movement developed alongside the efforts of state and local governments, but *not* the federal government, to address poverty. The federalist separation of power that had taken shape during the nineteenth century vested state and local governments with the responsibility to address poverty and other social problems, while the federal government retained control over fiscal matters such as banking, currency, and tariffs (Karl and Karl 1999; Karl and Katz 1981; Smith 1999).

A watershed moment that was to give longstanding legitimacy to the virtually total absence of federal control over policies concerning the poor had occurred several years earlier, in 1854. President Pierce vetoed a bill that Congress had passed which proposed various kinds of support for the mentally ill. The president justified his action by claiming that such federal involvement would be unconstitutional:

> I cannot find any authority in the Constitution for making the Federal Government the great almoner of public charity throughout the United States . . . [To do so] would be contrary to the letter and spirit of the

Constitution, and subversive of the whole theory upon which the union
of these states is founded (quoted in Trattner 1984: 66).

The federal government did briefly get involved in social welfare policy at
the end of the Civil War. In 1865 it created the Freedmen's Bureau, which
embarked on the massive task of helping the millions of emancipated
slaves—most of whom were uneducated and lacked job skills—to become
part of free society. Still, this move did not fundamentally alter the hands-
off posture that the federal government had assumed when it came to social
welfare issues. The federal government dismantled the Freedmen's Bureau
in 1872 and for the next several decades, policy matters concerning the
poor remained mostly in private and local hands. Congress attempted on
three separate occasions—in 1893–94, 1914, and 1921—to pass bills offering aid to the unemployed, yet each time the legislation encountered a presidential veto (Trattner 1984; Zarefsky 1986).

PRIVATE PHILANTHROPY AND THE GROWTH OF THE WELFARE STATE UNTIL THE 1960S

At the time that foundations started dispersing funds for research into the
causes of social problems, they were embarking into uncharted territory
given that the antipoverty efforts that had been previously undertaken—
whether privately or by state and local governments—had been aimed mostly
at relief, not reform. Foundation giving was innovative not only because its
aim was to redress social problems, but because in time it was to lay the
groundwork for a vastly expanded governmental role in social policy.

Early on, foundations funded social science research that historians
Barry and Alice Karl (1999: 58) aptly characterized as designed to keep
"the public abreast of problems and issues that the U.S. Congress would
not have considered touching with the proverbial ten-foot pole." Then,
during the Progressive Era, which lasted roughly from the turn of the twentieth century until World War I, this research became instrumental in bringing government attention for the first time to a host of social issues
concerning women, children, and manual workers. In particular, a group of
private reformers led by settlement house residents received support from
the Russell Sage Foundation for the "Pittsburgh Survey," which in six vol-
umes published between 1909 and 1914 documented the costs and consequences of low wages, poor health, and dilapidated housing within an
industrial city. The wide discussion and outrage generated by this report led
the foundation to fund similar studies of industrial problems in other cities
around the country. This foundation-inspired push for federal involvement

in social reform led to the creation of the Children's Bureau in 1912, and subsequently to the passage of federal child labor legislation (Trattner 1984).

Progressive reformers also succeeded in getting many states to pass laws enabling qualified mothers to receive pensions so that they could support their children without having to work long hours outside the home. Proponents of this legislation argued that public relief was needed to address the enormous financial burdens imposed by the layoff, family abandonment, extended illness, or death of a breadwinning husband. By 1935, all but two states (South Carolina and Georgia) had extended aid to women with children who lacked a husband's financial contribution to the household (Trattner 1984).

Hence, during the first three decades of the twentieth century a coalition of private interests consisting of foundations, settlement house residents, and social workers gradually succeeded in bringing the attention of the federal government to a variety of social issues that had previously been considered outside its domain. During the 1930s, the public sector's role in social policy expanded by leaps and bounds. The American welfare state became formally institutionalized amidst the unprecedented wave of "New Deal" legislation that President Franklin Roosevelt passed in the wake of the Great Depression. Through this legislation, the federal government for the first time provided social insurance for people who otherwise could not make ends meet. Between 1932 and 1939, government social welfare spending increased from $208 million to $4.9 billion (Katz 1995).

Social insurance took several forms. Roosevelt created the Federal Emergency Relief Administration, which provided rent, food, clothing, and medical care assistance to millions of people who suddenly found themselves out of work and in dire straits. Moreover, he signed into law the Social Security Act, which created old-age insurance and Aid to Dependent Children, a program that consolidated and expanded existing state widows' pension programs. Finally, since Roosevelt saw cash and in-kind assistance as a temporary response to an emergency, he created jobs through a number of new programs. The Public Works Administration provided jobs in construction. The Civilian Conservation Corps employed young men in reforestation, fire control, and flood prevention programs. And the Works Projects Administration employed displaced artists, musicians, and academics (Patterson 2000; Trattner 1984; Zarefsky 1986).

The New Deal signified a dramatic transformation of policymaking responsibility concerning America's poor. The provision of material relief, which was previously chiefly in either local or private hands, had for the past hundred years undergone criticism for helping the "undeserving" poor, who were seen as fully capable of improving their lot in life if they only tried a bit put forth a bit more personal initiative. But now sentiment concerning the poor had changed considerably. Whereas a political culture grounded in the Protestant work ethic and wedded to private and local reform initiatives had prevailed since the early days of colonial settlement in the New World, the Great Depression made two facts patently clear. First, poverty was not simply the individual's fault but rather was related to the structure of employment opportunities. Second, only the federal government could adequately respond to the massive amount of economic hardship that people were experiencing during the Depression. Private foundations simply did not have sufficient resources to adequately address this volume of need (Patterson 2000; Trattner 1984).

Although the massive expansion of the federal welfare state during the 1930s was due in part to foundations' being unequipped to deal with the hardship created by the Great Depression, it is important to emphasize that private philanthropy had laid the groundwork for welfare state expansion many years earlier. For indeed, foundation-sponsored research had brought attention to the structural underpinnings of a host of social problems, and consequently created a political climate in which now, for the first time in American history, it seemed appropriate for the federal government to become involved in social reform. Private interests and government had established an informal policymaking partnership that had legitimized the idea of a welfare state well before the Great Depression produced unprecedented levels of depravity begging for its creation.

During the years following World War II, foundations impacted social policy by launching reform initiatives that, when successful, often elicited the much greater funding resources of the public sector. For example, the National Institutes of Health modeled themselves on the medical and health-related research of several foundations, and the Rockefeller Foundation's fellowship programs for the advanced training of scientists became a model for the National Science Foundation. Even many years earlier, foundations had developed a distinctive capacity to leverage government support for new policy initiatives. For example, the Carnegie Foundation's major bequests to public libraries gradually led to the long-term support of library educational services by local governments around the country. Indeed, foundations' definitive accomplishment up through the 1970s was their ability to provide seed money for pilot projects that would subsequently become incorporated into public policy and funded on a much larger scale. Because of their abundant resources and their independence from the vested political and financial interests of government and business respectively, foundations were particularly well suited to play this role (Arnove 1980; Frumkin 1999; Nielsen 1985; Lenkowsky 1999).

THE HEYDAY OF FOUNDATION-GOVERNMENT PARTNERSHIP

The partnership between foundations and the federal government took important new directions during the 1960s. Leveraging occurred not only through foundation grants but also through the networks that policy specialists within the Kennedy and Johnson administrations fostered with their counterparts in the foundation world. The extent of philanthropists' and politicians' mutual interests was unprecedented. They included health, education, civil rights, urban renewal, legal services, environmental protection, voter registration, and product safety. The foundation-government partnership reached its zenith with the war on poverty, which began as a couple of demonstration projects funded by the Ford Foundation during the Kennedy years and subsequently received much more extensive federal support by the Johnson administration (Nielsen 1985; Lenkowsky 1999).

The first of these projects was the Gray Areas program, which the Ford Foundation initiated in 1961. The foundation viewed the existing social welfare bureaucracy's incoherent delivery of services as unequipped to meet the needs of the escalating number of poor blacks, Latinos, and Appalachian whites migrating to the "gray areas" between the central cities and suburbs. The central goal of the Gray Areas program was for youth to acquire the skills needed to compete for jobs in the urban labor market. Whereas during earlier eras poor newcomers to the city would gradually assimilate and adopt values that could foster social mobility, Ford's grants were based on the view that this opportunity structure no longer existed within poor urban neighborhoods, making youths susceptible to criminal behavior. The foundation's orientation was grounded in a number of sociological studies documenting that juvenile delinquency was a product *not* of individual pathology but of community disorganization. The most influential of these studies was Richard Cloward and Lloyd Ohlin's *Delinquency and Opportunity*. Published in 1960, this book argued that amidst the exodus of industry and white middle class residents from the inner city, and with the inadequacies of urban schools and social welfare agencies, poor youth lacked legitimate pathways for achieving conventional success, such as education, extracurricular activities, and part-time jobs. Juvenile delinquency was, therefore, a response to blocked opportunities (Halpern 1995; Katz 1989; O'Connor 1989).

By 1965, the Ford Foundation had spent $26.5 million on its Gray Areas program, dispersing grants to intermediary nonprofit organizations in five different cities: Boston, Philadelphia, New Haven, Oakland, and Washington, D.C. Each of these organizations was responsible for coordinating service delivery within a designated poor neighborhood and was then supposed to leverage other sources of funding. Indeed, many succeeded in doing so from the federal government—either from the Department of Labor or the President's Committee on Juvenile Delinquency and Youth Crime (Halpern 1995).

Cloward and Ohlin's book played an even more central role in the Ford Foundation's support for Mobilization for Youth, the second of its demonstration projects that served as a building block for the federal government's war on poverty. Begun in 1962, this program sought to address the growing gang problem on New York City's Lowest East Side, and did so in a manner similar to the Gray Areas program. Mobilization for Youth was a new intermediary organization created to coordinate service delivery to poor residents. One key difference was that under this program teachers were to act as positive role models for youth, trying to foster youth identification with their communities. Another difference was that the project advocated that poor residents actively participate in working to create institutional change within their neighborhood's service delivery system. The Ford Foundation contributed $12 million to Mobilization for Youth, and the organization leveraged other monies from the President's Committee on Juvenile Delinquency and Youth Crime, the National Institute of Mental Health, and New York City (Halpern 1995; O'Connor 1999).

As the Ford Foundation was escalating its commitments to both the Gray Areas project and Mobilization for Youth, it was gradually discovering shortcomings in its strategy of social reform. People within the foundation were beginning to question whether the problems they were targeting went beyond juvenile delinquency, and wondered how transforming the delivery of social services would change the opportunity structure. A Ford Foundation summary document issued in 1962 stated that "obstacles to economic and social betterment among low-income groups [were] responsible for delinquency." Moreover, it claimed that community participation in reforms was crucial "rather than have them imposed from without by persons who are alien to the traditions and aspirations of the community" (quoted in Katz 1989: 97). Internal criticism of the effectiveness of the foundation's programs for targeting juvenile delinquency reached its zenith during early 1963, which was the same time that the Kennedy administration was beginning to give serious consideration to putting its full weight behind a comprehensive poverty reform agenda (O'Connor 1999).

Up until this point, Kennedy had made several piecemeal efforts to ameliorate poverty. Unlike the social welfare legislation passed during the

1930s, Kennedy's policies placed a strong emphasis on expanding social service delivery in order to enhance poor people's commitment to the idea of hard work. In 1961 he created the President's Committee on Juvenile Delinquency and Youth Crime, which funded the Gray Areas project and Mobilization for Youth after each had accumulated evidence of being successful experimental programs. That same year Kennedy also signed into law the Area Redevelopment Act, which pumped $300 million into economically depressed regions throughout the country. The following year the Manpower Development and Training Act was enacted to provide job training to people who were chronically unemployed. In 1962, the Kennedy administration also implemented the Public Welfare Amendments, which provided up to five years of Aid to Families with Dependent Children benefits to two-parent families whose primary wage earner was out of work and no longer entitled to receive unemployment benefits. This legislation also increased federal funding to the states for services to public aid recipients that included job training, job placement, and casework (Patterson 2000; Trattner 1984).

During the spring and summer of 1963, the Kennedy administration framed comprehensive poverty reform as a major issue in its 1964 reelection platform. Influencing the administration's priorities were not only the Ford Foundation's funding of the Gray Areas project and Mobilization for Youth, but also the growing attention that social scientists and journalists had been giving to poverty since the late 1950s. In addition to Cloward and Ohlin's research, Michael Harrington's *The Other America,* published in 1962, was influential in raising public awareness about the deplorable conditions so many poor people encountered living within what was purportedly the richest country in the world (Waddan 1997).

Following the assassination of President Kennedy in November 1963, Lyndon Johnson continued to push for a comprehensive poverty reform agenda. His administration began to see the two demonstration projects funded by the Ford Foundation as no longer works in progress that allowed room for experimentation but as models for federal social policy. In his State of the Union address in January 1964, Johnson declared an "unconditional war on poverty" and the following August he signed the Economic Opportunity Act, which allocated $1 billion to a new independent federal agency—the Office of Economic Opportunity—to carry out the antipoverty agenda (Katz 1986; O'Connor 1999; Trattner 1984; Waddan 1997).

President Johnson's antipoverty program had two core agendas: *equal opportunity* and *community action.* The equal opportunity agenda emphasized expanding social services for the poor—particularly in the areas of education and job training—so that the poor could be more competitive in the labor market. Rather than directly transfer cash to the poor, as was the aim of the Aid to Families with Dependent Children entitlement, the ethos of the war on poverty was to offer the poor better access to opportunities for escaping poverty; in other words, helping the poor to help themselves. The Johnson administration referred to its poverty program as "a hand up, not a handout." The equal opportunity agenda had several components. For example, Operation Head Start provided an enriched education to preschool children and the Job Corps enabled high school dropouts to live in residential centers where they would learn industrial job skills (Trattner 1984).

The community action agenda opened up another kind of opportunity, calling for the "maximum feasible participation" of poor residents in both defining the scope of these new services and how best to deliver them. Whereas new education and job training programs aimed to give poor people greater access to economic opportunity, the ethos behind the community action program was that the poor could only take advantage of these opportunities if they directly had a say in creating them (Katz 1989; Patterson 2000; Waddan 1997).

THE WAR ON POVERTY COMES UNDER ATTACK

From its inception, the war on poverty was criticized because of fears by city politicians about what "maximum feasible participation" might mean, and about what it did in fact entail in some cities. Many mayors criticized the Johnson administration for creating a policy that funneled monies to community action agencies to use as they saw fit without being subjected to the traditional controls city governments exercised over local purse strings. Some mayors consequently saw the community action program as a vehicle for the federal government to permit the poor to defy local political institutions, and consequently ignite class antagonisms (Patterson 2000; Waddan 1997).

These criticisms greatly diminished the optimism toward comprehensive poverty reform that existed within the Johnson administration during 1964 and 1965. Not only was the political tide turning against community action but the Vietnam War was also increasingly consuming the administration's attention. As early as December 1965, presidential aides had recommended that the administration consider scaling down the war on poverty by eliminating the Office of Economic Opportunity and parceling out its functions to other federal departments, such as the newly created Department of Housing and Urban Development and Department of Labor. Although President Johnson did not follow through on these recommendations, several years later his successor to the Oval Office, Richard Nixon, did embrace similar measures (Lemann 1981; Patterson 2000).

The Johnson administration's scaling down of the war on poverty proceeded along two fronts. In 1966 Congress instituted the Model Cities program, which the administration saw as an improvement on, and in time essentially as a replacement for, community action. This program shifted the central idea promoted by the community action program—empowering the poor to initiate poverty reforms—into the concept of community development, whereby the goal was to turn poor neighborhoods into middle-class ones. While the Model Cities program did similarly emphasize citizen participation, it did so in ways that assured that municipal governments would clearly be in control this time around. The Department of Housing and Urban Development, not the Office of Economic Opportunity, administered the Model Cities program. Initially conceived as a demonstration program, Model Cities expanded within two years to include 150 cities (Lemann 1981).

In 1967, the Johnson administration made another retreat from the community action program through its support of the "Green Amendment." Proposed by Representative Edith Green of Oregon, this legislation designated that states, counties, or cities serve as community action agencies unless these entities preferred instead to select a nonprofit organization, and stipulated that one-third of agency board members be public officials. After extensive debate, the amendment passed. It actually produced little noticeable change since there already was considerable representation by local politicians within community action agencies. The Green Amendment's significance was instead mostly symbolic, for it publicly legitimized the Johnson administration's retreat from its earlier focus on the maximum feasible participation of the poor in effecting comprehensive poverty reform (Zarefsky 1986).

Among the reasons for Richard Nixon's triumph in the 1968 presidential election was a growing belief among the American public that the unprecedented liberal expansion of the welfare state that took place under the Johnson administration was both ill-conceived and actually did more harm than good. Criticism of the war on poverty had begun, as we have seen, while Lyndon Johnson was still in office, indeed soon after the implementation of the Economic Opportunity Act of 1964. And, for several years that criticism focused specifically on the community action program. But, as the sixties drew to a close, this criticism gradually transformed into a broader de-legitimation of federal involvement in social policy. This transformation signified the ascendance of neo-conservatism and with it a fundamental ideological re-orientation of American social policy, a monumental shift whose effects remain salient to this very day.

Within the Nixon administration, there was considerable skepticism about the merits of the war on poverty. Daniel Patrick Moynihan, a social scientist and one of the first outspoken critics of the community action program, was to have a profound effect on Nixon's handling of policy matters. Whereas a few years earlier Moynihan had been a supporter of the federal government's expanded role in social welfare policy, he came to share with Nixon a deep disdain for the liberalism of both the Kennedy and Johnson administrations. Despite Nixon's particular dislike for the war on poverty, Moynihan tactically advised the president to maintain the Office of Economic Opportunity and to increase the budget for Model Cities. During his first term in office, Nixon also supported a number of other liberal reform agendas. Among these were a program to create temporary jobs in urban ghettos, subsidized housing, block grants for cities, increased funding for Aid to Families with Dependent Children, and an expansion of the food stamps program. Aware that Nixon had assumed the Oval Office at a time of very strong liberal sentiment within Congress, the media, universities, foundations, and even much of the corporate world, Moynihan's strategy was for the administration to appear liberal in order to gradually co-opt the left and incrementally shift social policy toward the right (Lemann 1981).

The most salient illustration of Moynihan's maneuvers to disarm the left was the Nixon administration's Family Assistance Plan proposed in August 1969. This policy sought to elevate poor households with children—single-parent and two-parent families alike—above the poverty line by replacing Aid to Families with Dependent Children with a guaranteed income. The plan resembled the Work Incentive Program created by President Johnson two years earlier in that both measures promoted "workfare" by requiring adult recipients to work or otherwise forfeit their cash transfer payments. Moynihan pitched this proposal to Nixon as cheap in that it would replace the Johnson administration's services-based attack on poverty with an income-based approach, thereby substantially trimming the federal social welfare bureaucracy. Moynihan believed that even if liberals criticized this plan for its conservative cost cutting, the proposal would trump the Left by building on an earlier Johnson administration program and by guaranteeing to eradicate poverty—a claim that none of Johnson's antipoverty programs could meet (Lemann 1981; Patterson 2000; Trattner 1984).

The Family Assistance Plan encountered intense resistance from conservative Democrats, who proceeded to block its passage. They saw this plan as creating even greater welfare dependency than Aid to Families with Dependent Children, which had undergone intensifying criticism during the 1960s for precisely that reason. Moynihan did not contest this claim but rather saw creating permanent welfare dependency as an acceptable state of affairs if accompanied by a divestment from service-based social welfare spending for the poor. Congress did, however, enact a law in 1971 that expanded the workfare requirements of the Work Incentive Program, stipulating that all adult recipients of Aid to Families with Dependent Children except mothers with children under six had to register for job training programs (Lemann 1981; Patterson 2000; Trattner 1984).

Upon winning re-election in 1972, President Nixon became less content with simply disarming his liberal critics and more intent on taking decisive steps to dismantle the war on poverty. He began to transfer Lyndon Johnson's various service-based initiatives from the Office of Economic Opportunity to other federal departments. Project Head Start went to the Department of Health, Education, & Welfare and the Job Corps to the Department of Labor. Nixon also set in motion what became known as the "new federalism."—an effort by the federal government to reverse a trend that had increasingly, from the Roosevelt through the Johnson administrations, transferred responsibility for social policy from localities and private interests to the welfare state. In 1973, Nixon enacted the Comprehensive Employment and Training Act, which consolidated the various federal job-training programs instituted during the Johnson years and gave authority to local governments to administer them. For cities with populations over 100,000, the federal government allocated a single lump sum to local governments, and for job training in more sparsely populated areas the federal government gave lump sums to the states (Patterson 2000; Trattner 1984).

Nixon also had plans for phasing out the war on poverty's community action program. He proposed replacing the Office of Economic Opportunity with a newly created Community Services Administration, which would coordinate remaining community action agencies within the Department of Health, Education, & Welfare. Nixon never implemented this plan due to his resignation from office following the Watergate scandal. However, soon after assuming the Oval Office, Gerald Ford enacted the measure. During the remainder of his truncated term in office, Ford extended the fiscal conservatism that Nixon had displayed after being reelected, by vetoing federal aid to education and health care, a federal public works bill, and a school lunch program (Katz 1986; Lemann 1981; Trattner 1984).

THE NEW RIGHT'S ASCENDANCE TO POLITICAL POWER

Even though Ford vetoed a number of liberal social reforms, a growing neo-conservative wing of the Republican Party was beginning to attack both him and Nixon for not vehemently taking a stand against liberal stances on a number of issues. These included not only poverty and welfare but also abortion, women's rights, the environment, school busing, and affirmative action. In the eyes of these neo-conservatives, Nixon's and Ford's efforts under the "new federalism" to scale back federal involvement in a number of social programs was not a decisive enough stand against the liberal tide that had descended upon Washington since the Kennedy administration.

In Ronald Reagan, the neo-conservative movement found a formidable right-wing challenger to Gerald Ford in the 1976 Republican primary. Although Ford ultimately prevailed over Reagan, it is important to highlight the significant foothold within the Republican Party that the New Right had gained by the mid-seventies. It had succeeded in demarcating itself ideologically from the rest of the party by its stances on a number of social issues, differentiating itself from the old-line Republican focus on national security and free-market economics (Berman 1994).

In practice, the ideological differences between the New and Old Right were actually quite small. What distinguished the rise of the New Right was instead how a group of intellectuals re-packaged longstanding conservative views, and consequently used novel tactics to spur a broad-based social movement. The neo-conservative movement began during the 1950s through the publication of a number of prominent journals, most notably the *National Review*. During the early sixties, young activists began to attach themselves to this nascent movement by joining the John Birth Society or one of a number of newly created Christian-based right wing organizations. Activists also formed Young Americans for Freedom, which sought to galvanize young adults to become interested in conservative political candidates (Himmelstein 1990).

The 1964 presidential bid by Barry Goldwater was a pivotal moment in the early development of the New Right. Although Lyndon Johnson won the election decisively, Goldwater's campaign created an opportunity for young conservatives to become active in national politics and for those on the far right to gain a prominent voice within the Republican Party. Leading conservatives created the American Conservative Union to serve at the frontlines of the neo-conservative battleground. The membership of this organization, as well as Young Americans for Freedom, was continuing to grow by leaps and bounds (Himmelstein 1990).

By the late sixties, fractures within the Left were also contributing to the growing legitimacy of the New Right. Whereas there had previously been a broad liberal consensus supporting an expanded government role in targeting social problems, as a reaction to the radical sentiment expressed by black nationalists, antiwar protesters, and the hippie counterculture, many card-carrying liberals began to question their allegiance to the Democratic Party. Specifically concerning the radicalization of the civil rights movement, neo-conservative critics blamed the war on poverty's community action program for fostering urban violence and turmoil while at the same time not doing much to help the poor escape poverty.

Daniel Patrick Moynihan's shift in political allegiances and forging of close ties with the Republican ticket that won the 1968 presidential election was, as we have seen, a salient illustration of the diverse appeal that neo-conservative criticism of the war on poverty was attracting. Contemporary public discourse generally overlooked the fact that most community action programs functioned without political controversy and achieved some meaningful results. Instead, Moynihan both reflected and contributed to the mounting attack on the war on poverty when he published in 1969 *Maximum Feasible Misunderstanding*, a critical history of the community action program (Zarefsky 1986).

Neo-conservative critics were increasingly framing the war on poverty as emblematic of a flawed liberal impulse to "throw money at the problem," claiming that the federal government had spent billions of dollars on social programs during the 1960s and yet millions of Americans still remained poor. The growing support that neo-conservatism was receiving during the late sixties meant that Richard Nixon had assumed the Oval Office amidst a political climate well suited to enticing Democratic loyalists—namely white southerners, Catholics, and blue-collar workers—to switch their allegiances to the Republican Part, which was in fact what happened during the 1972 reelection of President Nixon (Adler 1994; Himmelstein 1990; Katz 1989; Trattner 1984; Waddan 1997).

This belief that big government could not ameliorate social problems but was *itself* a problem in need of fixing became an instrumental rallying cry in the New Right's rise to prominence during the late 1970s. In the meantime the neo-conservative movement had its work cut out for itself. The Republican Party suddenly faced a monumental crisis when, in August 1974, President Nixon resigned from office over the Watergate scandal. The information that came out concerning the extent of the Nixon administration's efforts to unduly influence the results of the 1972 election disgraced the Party, set back the New Right agenda several years, and contributed toward Jimmy Carter's triumph in the 1976 presidential election. Once again, a Democrat was in the White House. As Carter worked to bring a liberal antipoverty reform agenda back to Washington, the neo-conservative movement began to re-organize its forces, strengthen its networks, and build up its financial base in preparation for the 1980 presidential campaign (Himmelstein 1990).

Carter attempted to reconcile his liberal social policy agenda with the neo-conservative fervor that permeated around him. He made a strong effort to claim, for example, that federal government policies were partially responsible for the soaring inflation rates that accompanied his term in office. Although Carter tacitly embraced what by the mid 1970s had become *de rigeour* rhetoric within conservative circles—that there were limits to the government's capacity to solve social problems—he nonetheless attempted to pass what was arguably the most liberal federal antipoverty reform proposal to date: the Better Jobs and Income Program.

This proposal called for replacing all existing social welfare programs with a two-tiered initiative: a jobs program for the 1.4 million able-bodied people who were unemployed and a guaranteed income for those who were unable to work. This proposal differed from Nixon's failed Family Assistance Plan in four respects: it applied to all poor people (not just families), its income benefits were greater, there were more work exemptions allowed for women with children, and it had a substantial jobs component. And it was these differences that assured that the Better Jobs and Income Program would experience the same fate as Nixon's Family Assistance Plan. President Carter simply could not shake the conservative resolve within Congress to trim social spending and not touch with a ten-foot pole antipoverty reforms that appeared comprehensive in scope. Indeed, it was this combination—policies that were both comprehensive and costly—that by the end of Carter's term in office neo-conservatives were coherently framing as the central flaw of liberal antipoverty policy (Berman 1994; Trattner 1984).

As the 1970s drew to a close, the New Right had amassed a tremendous amount of organizational and financial clout. A well-developed neo-conservative institutional apparatus existed consisting of foundations, think tanks, public policy research institutes, and intellectual publications such as *Commentary, The Public Interest,* and *National Review.* There was, as well, an extensive set of networks forged on college campuses, enabling young people to train for and become actively involved in the neo-conservative movement (Nielsen 1985).

A RETURN TO THE "GOOD 'OLE DAYS"

The formal political triumph of the New Right took place with the landslide presidential victory of Ronald Reagan in 1980. The so-called "Reagan Revolution" that unfolded during the ensuring eight years reflected, among other things, the strong neo-conservative sentiment that had crystallized during the seventies about how government antipoverty programs initiated by Presidents Kennedy and Johnson were colossal failures. As we have seen, the dominant rhetoric within neo-conservative intellectual circles was that during the sixties the federal government "threw money at the problem" and that it was now time to massively scale back government social programs (Berman 1994).[1]

While rhetoric about the evils of big government had for some time been steadily gaining public support, in Ronald Reagan the New Right finally had a man vested by the electorate with the political power to act upon that rhetoric. The Reagan Revolution consisted of a series of massive budget cuts aimed to reduce the waste and inefficiency that the administration saw as emblematic of the growth in the welfare state that occurred during the 1960s. The Reagan administration's sentiment concerning social policy was perhaps best characterized by David Stockman, Director of the Office of Management and Budget, who commented in reference to his hometown of Benton Harbor, Michigan:

> I wouldn't be surprised if $100 million had been spent here in the last twenty years. Urban renewal, CETA (Comprehensive Employment and Training Act), Model Cities, they've had everything. And the results? No impact whatsoever (quoted in Lemann 1981: 219).

Upon assuming office, President Reagan quickly acted upon his campaign pledge to make across-the-board cuts in social spending. He engaged in a general effort to defund the Left by not allowing federal funds to go to nonprofits that advocated outwardly liberal agendas. Concerning the poor specifically, his single biggest cut was in the jobs program under the Comprehensive Employment and Training Act. Moreover, he significantly scaled back VISTA, the domestic federal program that sent volunteers into poor communities, and completely eliminated the Community Services Administration, which had previously been the Office of Economic Opportunity—the administrative engine of the war on poverty (Lemann 1981; Nielsen 1985; Trattner 1984).

In making these sweeping cuts, Reagan sought to stake out the moral high ground concerning the poor. He heralded the downsizing of government as a way of ensuring that public assistance went to those who truly needed it rather than to freeloaders who could easily find jobs or to professional bureaucrats who siphoned off funds from welfare programs that were supposed to benefit the poor. Moreover, in creating the President's Task Force on Private Sector Initiatives, Reagan heralded private philanthropy as a superior mechanism than the federal government for ameliorating poverty since private giving did not breed the waste and inefficiency that had become endemic to government social programs. In short, the administration sought nothing less than a fundamental transformation of responsibility for social policy from the federal government to the private sector (Boris 1999; Lenkowsky 1999).

Reagan's successor, George Bush, similarly advocated privatization as the appropriate way to target poverty and other social problems. His "Thousand Points of Light" initiative called both for a greater share of responsibility for social welfare to be shouldered by nonprofit organizations and for individuals to become more involved in helping those less fortunate than themselves. Bush claimed that if these goals were fulfilled, his initiative would become "the most comprehensive and inclusive movement of our time" (quoted in Cloud 1991: 51).

It is noteworthy how the Republican administrations that occupied the Oval Office throughout the eighties and early nineties rhetorically legitimized transferring responsibility for social policy from the federal government to the private sector. Consider, for example, this claim made by Ronald Reagan during his first term in office:

> Before government was the principle vehicle of social change (in other words, before the creation of the welfare state during the 1930s), it was understood that the real source of our progress as a people was the private sector" (quoted in Nielsen 1985: 48).

Hence, the Reagan Revolution, on whose coattails much of George Bush's social policy agenda rested, was premised upon a return to a better time in our history. This was a time when there was a tradition in place of private and local solutions to problems of economic hardship; a tradition that unraveled due to the misguided liberal expansion of the federal government that began under Franklin Roosevelt and continued through the Johnson years. For Reagan and Bush, reclaiming this tradition was a powerful move given how culturally disposed Americans are toward viewing charitable giving as a more appropriate vehicle than government for addressing social needs. This move was a way of simultaneously garnering support for the neo-conservative attack on big government and pointing to a better means of targeting poverty that tapped into a tradition "as American as apple pie" (Karl and Karl 1999; Loseke 1997). [2]

At the same time that the Reagan and Bush administrations were both applauding private philanthropy as a replacement for government reforms, these administrations were leveling an attack on foundations. In particular, Reagan criticized liberal foundations, like the Ford Foundation, whose work had been instrumental in the creation of the war on poverty. The President and his aides viewed the grantmaking of liberal-leaning foundations as prone to incite hostility and radical sentiment as well as to seeding the core problem the Reagan Revolution sought to eradicate: big government. Indeed, under Reagan the foundation-government partnership that had been the engine of liberal social reform since the 1930s was systematically dismantled. The federal government continued to maintain close ties with foundations but of a very different political stripe: those that funded research produced and disseminated by conservative think tanks such as the Heritage Foundation (Nielsen 1985).

Even prior to Reagan's presidency, these think tanks had become instrumental in re-shaping the ways that politicians were conceptualizing the problem of poverty and what should be done about it. Neo-conservative intellectuals like Charles Murray and Lawrence Mead charged that federal antipoverty programs initiated during the sixties promoted abuse of the welfare system and caused single mothers to become welfare dependent. Indeed, *welfare dependency*—not poverty—was gradually becoming the core problem that politicians saw as in need of fixing (Schram 1995; Weaver 2000).

This re-framing of the poverty problem in terms of welfare dependency subsequently guided federal social policy throughout the eighties and early nineties, and ultimately became instrumental in shaping the monumental federal welfare reform legislation passed in 1996. The powerful influence of neo-conservative ideology is highlighted by the fact that a *Democratic* president, Bill Clinton, signed this reform into law. Indeed, so much of the neo-conservative spin about poverty and welfare had become conventional political wisdom during the Reagan and Bush years that no Democrat could realistically mount a credible presidential campaign without embracing it. While Bill Clinton certainly espoused liberal ideas on a number of issues, he won the 1992 presidential election in no small part because he presented himself as a *New Democrat* committed to "ending welfare as we knew it" (Weaver 2000).

The specific content of the welfare reform law—the Personal Responsibility and Work Opportunity Reconciliation Act of 1996—reflects the extent to which Clinton had to reckon with the dramatic outcomes of the 1994 congressional elections. Republicans gained the majority in both the House and Senate for the first time since the 1946 midterm election, and proceeded to chart a course for a major reorganization of the federal government, which they spelled out in their "Contract with America." It called for continued downsizing of the federal government through *devolution*, the shifting of policy responsibilities to state and local governments, as well as increased responsibility placed on private philanthropy for addressing social problems (Alexander 1999; Schram 2000; Wolpert 1997).

FOUNDATION-INITIATED ANTIPOVERTY REFORM
IN AN ERA OF GOVERNMENT DOWNSIZING

In overhauling the social welfare system that had been in place since the 1930s, welfare reform substantially contributed toward achieving the neo-conservative goal to transform responsibility for the making of social policy. The federal government now devolved much of this work to state and local governments, and expected more from private philanthropy. Embedded within these shifts was the notion that the policy role that the federal government now ought to be playing was as an enabler, rather than an initiator, of social reform (Deakin 2001; Lenkowsky 1999).

Many politically liberal foundations, which for several decades had become accustomed to partnering with the federal government to promote antipoverty reforms, now had to redefine their policymaking roles. The most dramatic response these foundations made in the wake of the federal government's downsizing of its role in social policy during the 1980s and 1990s was their sponsorship of comprehensive community initiatives. In some instances city governments partnered with foundations in funding these initiatives, however in *no* cases was the federal government involved—a reflection of the transformed policy milieu in which these initiatives came about (Brown and Garg 1997; Walsh 1997).

It is ironic that liberal foundations were a central target of the neo-conservative assault on government-sponsored social reform, and yet they mounted little resistance toward this policy transformation that began with the Reagan Revolution and became solidified through welfare reform. Quite to the contrary, despite the ideological divide between these foundations and the neo-conservatives at the forefront of reconfiguring the social policy landscape during the eighties and nineties, these foundations generally embraced the neo-conservative call for private and local solutions to poverty (Lenkowsky 1999; O'Connor 1999).

The distinguishing characteristic of comprehensive community initiatives that is pertinent to the narrative about the Chicago Initiative that unfolds in the next three chapters is that these initiatives were the central institutional mechanism of antipoverty policy during an era of massive welfare state downsizing. The fact that comprehensive community initiatives existed in nearly every major U.S. city at some point during the eighties and nineties is evidence of their strong presence as a vehicle for antipoverty reform. Moreover, these initiatives were often in dialogue with one another, exchanging information and coordinating their efforts through the Bay Area-based National Community Building Network.

Comprehensive community initiatives gained an institutional presence within a political climate in which there was a level of ideological support for private and local poverty reform that had not existed since *before* the first private foundations were established in the latter part of the 19th century. These initiatives were an illustration of just how closely late 20th century U.S. social policy resembled the state of affairs that existed up until the creation of the welfare state during the first third of the 20th century.

Section II
Venturing Inside the Chicago Initiative

Chapter Three
Organizational Motivations for Sponsorship

Although comprehensive community initiatives assumed a common institutional form due to the political climate in which they arose during the 1980s and 1990s, each came into being through circumstances unique to the particular local context. This chapter focuses on the story that unfolded in Chicago beginning in the spring of 1992 following the LA riots. After discussing the fears that fueled the creation of the Chicago Initiative, I broaden the discussion by pointing out parallels between foundations' motivations for sponsoring this initiative and the similar motivations of foundations supporting comprehensive community initiatives across other U.S. cities.

FEARING A LONG, HOT SUMMER

In producing grisly media images of heavy casualties and widespread destruction of property, the LA riots rekindled deep-seated memories of the successive years of turbulence that plagued so many American cities during the 1960s, none more so than Chicago. Indeed, Chicago is the city that many observers and commentators most often associate with the history of recurrent urban racial violence. The various institutions that took part in the Chicago Initiative were motivated by a riveting sense of fear that the city might experience a snowball of what was currently taking place in LA—and a replay of Chicago's own violent past—unless they came up with a plan for keeping peace on the streets during what could otherwise become an especially long and hot summer.

Embedded within the collective memory of those that banded together to create the Chicago Initiative in May 1992 was a deep recognition of

Chicago's racially divisive history. One of the bloodiest riots in American history took place in the city over a span of five days during July 1919. Thirty-eight people died and 537 were injured (Chicago Initiative 1993a). Forty-five years later during the summer of 1964, Chicago was one of six Northern cities to experience riots. That year marked the beginning of an unprecedented five-year period of racial violence across American cities, including Chicago, Detroit, Los Angeles, New York, Baltimore, Washington, D.C., and Philadelphia (Hubbard 1968).

There was another riot on Chicago's West Side in the summer of 1966 which, despite the extensive damage, actually paled in comparison to the unparalleled racial violence that took place across U.S. cities following the assassination of Dr. Martin Luther King, Jr. by a white sniper in Memphis on April 4, 1968. During the ensuing two weeks, widespread rioting occurred in Baltimore, Washington, D.C., and most notably in Chicago, resulting in over forty deaths (Farber 1988; Masotti et al. 1969).

Immediately after the King assassination, the streets of Chicago were quiet and remained that way into the next morning. During the afternoon, as people in Garfield Park, a few miles west of downtown, listened to speakers mourn Dr. King, the mood changed. Students from Austin High School marched down Madison Street in what started out as a peaceful protest. Then, some broke rank. Hundreds—eventually thousands—of black youth proceeded to smash windows and loot the almost entirely white-owned stores. Even some blacks that did not closely identify with Dr. King participated in the riots (Chicago Initiative 1993a; Farber 1988; Haines 1988.

Dormant memories of these recurring episodes of racial violence resurfaced in the minds of many concerned Chicago citizens in the immediate aftermath of the 1992 LA riots, producing a riveting sense of fear. The LA riots did not just forewarn about potentially comparable violence that might take place in Chicago. The riots, moreover, brought to the forefront of people's minds images of the long, difficult history of race relations in the city; images that were especially powerful with regard to the racial violence of the 1960s.[1]

One of Chicago's prominent religious leaders, who also served as chairman of the board of the Chicago Fund, the foundation that spearheaded the Chicago Initiative, described in an interview how the LA riots rekindled disturbing memories of the racial violence of the 1960s and provoked fears of a snowball effect in Chicago that summer.

> The state of race relations is always tender in this city. And it has been ever since I've been here—since the mid 50s. And all you need is—and of course the city had gone through riots in the past, and who would have thought that this incident starting with the Rodney King beating would

turn out to be the kind of situation that it turned out to be in that riot in California. I know from having once patrolled the streets during riots that once it gets on, there is very little you can do to get people to be rational. I think that the first riot I ever experienced in Chicago came about because during the hot summer, kids turned on the fire hydrants, like they always do, and the police came and turned them off. And kids turned them on again and then the police came and before you knew it you had an alter- cation out there on the West Side. And the next thing we knew, it was wholesale rioting, and Mayor [Richard J.] Daley called on the clergy to walk the streets. And that was the first time. But, once you get that thing out of control, what you have to do is restore order and bring in force to restore order. We did not want that to occur again in Chicago.

Among the foundations that joined together to create the Chicago Initia- tive in the days following the LA riots, concerns intensified when the superin- tendent of the Chicago Police Department came to an early meeting of the Initiative. Several funders described in interviews that the stark message he con- veyed at that meeting added to their growing sense that there were pent-up frustrations and anger in the city's poor neighborhoods that could boil over into acts of rage. Funders were especially fearful that after June 19, when the Chicago public schools' summer recess began, poor youth with time on their hands would be prone to violence. A staff person at the Chicago Fund described the sense of panic in the room that was evident by the conclusion of that meeting:

> It was like there was a powder keg out there, and I think those of us who lived in major urban cities around the country thought, "There, but for the grace of God, go we," and we weren't even sure that the grace of God was going to help us. And so the idea was, what could be done and what could be done on short notice?

Funders' fears additionally stemmed from the fact that Chicago still retained physical evidence of the 1968 riots. Many buildings on the city's West Side remained burned out, boarded up, and uninhabited. The neigh- borhood had only just recently begun to show small signs of revitalization with the building of the United Center for sporting events and concerts, and the opening of the James Jordan Boys and Girls Club (Chicago Initiative 1993a). Even despite these signs of revitalization, links between the West Side's history of riots and funders' fears of a new outbreak of racial vio- lence were all too real given that extensive looting within that neighbor- hood had indeed recently taken place, both after the Chicago Bulls won their first National Basketball Association championship in 1991 and again after their second championship in 1992.

The central image fueling funders' fears concerned the possible racial targeting of a new episode of local riots. There was a deeply embedded anxiety among the predominantly white foundation executive directors that an outbreak of violence in Chicago could pit blacks against whites, possibly threatening downtown business interests. The precise extent to which funders' fears of riots occurring in Chicago were racial was difficult for me to ascertain. In my interviews, funders often expressed concerns about violence occurring among "poor youth," "inner-city youth," or sometimes simply "youth"— euphemisms that left open the remote possibility that they perceived affluent white kids from the suburbs as posing an impending threat to the social order. My difficulty in documenting an explicit racial picture of funders' riot fears probably stemmed from their feeling uncomfortable articulating links between race and violence, since these links might get misconstrued as racist.

But, these links certainly existed, and indeed were embedded within the news media's extensive coverage of the LA riots (Hunt 1997). Through continuous replaying of both the Rodney King beating and the grisly violence that followed the acquittal of the four Los Angeles police officers who allegedly abused him, the news media significantly contributed to funders' fears. The King beating and LA riots were events that carried the kind of narrative appeal audiences typically want and fixate upon in news reports. In each case, there was a familiar cast of characters, a continuously unfolding drama, graphic video footage, and most notably fear-provoking imagery (Altheide 2002; Best 2003; Firestone 1999). The feared possibility of violence snowballing from LA to Chicago was, thus, a product of how the media framed the LA riots (Gamson and Modigliani 1989). The saturated, fear-inducing coverage of this story contributed toward depicting the riots in funders' minds as a crisis that demanded their immediate action.[2]

Indeed, media coverage of the riots contributed to funders' conception of the Chicago Initiative as a necessary effort on their part to avert a similar crisis from occurring locally. The director of the Chicago Fund, the person who originally devised the idea for the collaboration, claimed during the keynote address at the official kickoff meeting of the Chicago Initiative in June 1992.

> [W]e are deeply concerned as are many, many others that there will be very large numbers of inner-city youth and young adults with absolutely nothing constructive to do this summer. The LA riots attest to the substantial potential such a situation presents for a disaster. To do nothing but sit back and hope for the best is irresponsible (Chicago Initiative 1992a).

Another staff person at the Chicago Fund explicitly linked the impetus to spearhead the Chicago Initiative with the foundation's concerns about impending racial violence in the city.

> I think one of the things that happened was that the Los Angeles situation had been cast in strictly racial terms. And predating that, the [Chicago Fund] had done that study on racial and ethnic and religious tensions. So, there was a sort of heightened sense of, "Oh, we really ought to do something about race relations in this, the most segregated city in America."

KEEPING THE CITY "COOL"

The Chicago Initiative came into being in response to one driving question: "If it is true that tensions are running higher than usual this summer, then what can we do to cool a long, hot Chicago summer" (Chicago Initiative 1992b)? The collaboration adopted as its immediate goal to expand programming for poor youth while they were out of school for the summer and would otherwise have idle time on their hands that they might spend on the streets behaving disruptively. It is not unusual during the spring for foundations to focus their summer grantmaking on programs that provide structured activities for kids while school is in recess. Funders' particular concern in 1992 was that without a dramatic expansion of local recreational and employment opportunities, poor youth would be particularly prone to violence given what had transpired in Los Angeles (Chicago Initiative 1992b).

To meet this goal of expanding summer opportunities for poor youth, the executive director of the Chicago Fund gave an initial pledge of $1.15 million from his foundation, and proceeded to solicit contributions from other foundations throughout the city. In an interview, he described how he pitched the imperative for other foundations to support the Chicago Initiative.

> When I went to them and said, "All the [social service] agencies are really worried that this summer, there's going to be a blow-up, not unlike LA, and people are really mad, and hot, and all of that," they understood what I meant. And they said, "Yeah. Here's some money. Let's see if you can at least cool it down a little bit."

In total, twenty-seven foundations pooled together $2.7 million for the Chicago Initiative to distribute to community-based organizations serving poor youth during the summer of 1992. Twenty of these funders were corporate, while the remaining seven were independent. However, as Table 3 shows, independent foundations contributed the majority of the money.[3]

Table 3: Foundation Contributions to the Chicago Initiative's 1992 Summer Grants
Campaign

Type	Number	Dollars given (% of total)
Corporate	20	600,000 (22%)
Independent	7	2,100,000 (78%)
Total	27	2,700,000 (100%)

(This material originally appeared in Ira Silver, *Nonprofit and Voluntary Sector Quarterly*
33(4):606–27. © 2004 by Sage Publications. Reprinted by permission of Sage Publications.)

Four task forces were created to evaluate grant proposals across a
range of programming areas deemed important for aiding poor youth.
These were Sports & Recreation, Arts & Culture, Gang Intervention, and
Jobs/Job Training. The goal of each task force was to read grant proposals
submitted by community-based organizations across the city and make
grant recommendations for programs that expanded summer employment
and recreational opportunities for poor youth (Chicago Initiative 1992b).

Between 12–40 people served on these task forces. As Table 4 indicates,
63 percent were from community-based organizations while the rest were
either foundation staff, representatives from city agencies, or other policy
advocates. It was significant that community-based organizations were in the
majority since this enabled them to wield an influence over grantmaking that
they seldom exercise. In those situations where there was a potential conflict
of interest concerning a task force member's evaluation of his/her own organization's grant proposal, that person did not exercise a vote.

Table 4: Participation on the Chicago Initiative's Summer Task Forces

Program	Community-based organizations	City agency	Foundations	Other policy advocates	Total
Sports & Recreation	13	2	2	2	19
Arts & Culture	11	3	1	1	16
Jobs/Job Training	23	3	5	9	40
Gang Intervention	8	3	1	0	12
TOTAL:	55 (63%)	11 (13%)	9 (10%)	12 (14%)	87 (100%)

(This material originally appeared in Ira Silver, *Nonprofit and Voluntary Sector Quarterly*
33(4):606–27. © 2004 by Sage Publications. Reprinted by permission of Sage Publications.)

Grant recommendations were then sent to the Distributions Committee, which consisted of those funders that donated at least $50,000 to the Chicago Initiative. Over 95 percent of the time, this committee approved the task forces' recommendations. The committee allocated all of its available funds within just six weeks of receiving grant proposals, and the time it took from grant approval to the processing of checks was just one day (Chicago Initiative 1992c).

While funders each had one vote on this committee, they did not all exercise equal influence over the Initiative's future courses of action. Those that contributed the highest amounts generally had more say and the Chicago Fund, as the leader of the collaboration, had the most say of all. There were also at-large, non-voting members of the committee representing business, labor, clergy, and city government (Chicago Initiative 1992b).

Most of the $2.4 million allocated to community-based organizations during the summer of 1992 supported programs for poor African Americans and Latinos living on Chicago's South and West Sides, in the Cabrini-Green Housing Development on the Near North Side, and in the Uptown neighborhood on the North Side (Chicago Initiative 1993a). Since there was an overall emphasis placed on creating employment opportunities, the Jobs/Job Training Task Force targeted a piece of its funding specifically to 12–15 year olds. This age group was neither eligible for the city's federal summer jobs money under the Job Training Partnership Act nor for a separate summer jobs program run by the civic organization Concerned Corporate Leaders (Chicago Initiative 1992f).

The general focus of all summer programs was to keep youth busy, since idle time might lead to unrest. Jobs were intended both to provide a sense of purpose and to leave little room for unstructured, potentially destructive activity. For this reason, one of the programs that funders hailed most was giving social-service agencies money to keep their gymnasiums open until midnight for kids to play late-night basketball. Instead of being on the streets and possibly involved in disruptive activity, youth would be kept busy and would become exhausted through their physical activity. Supporting midnight basketball reflected funders' fear that in the absence of having constructive recreational activities, clusters of energetic youth might roam the streets late at night and engage in violent behavior.

The link between funders' fears of riots and the summer programs they endorsed is perhaps best illustrated by a grant proposal that they ended up not supporting. On May 26, 1992, just three weeks after the Initiative was conceived, Mayor Richard M. Daley asked the Chicago Park District "to develop something for the many children living in the State Street developments" (Chicago Initiative 1992g). He was referring to a cluster of segregated public housing high rises on Chicago's South Side that comprise one of the poorest black census tracts in the country (Massey and Denton 1993). The Park District devised a proposal asking for half a million dollars to bus kids downtown to Grant Park for athletic competitions. The coordinator of the Chicago Initiative's 1992 summer programs explained that the Distribution Committee rejected the proposal for two reasons. First, the mayor could have asked the Chicago Transit Authority directly to absorb the cost of busing these kids. And second, these kids already had access to the downtown park facilities. It is additionally revealing what she mentioned in an interview, seemingly as an afterthought:

> And then they wanted to have the orange shirts playing the red shirts, and I said "you know, guys you're getting ready to set up some turf that nobody's going to be able to facilitate." And, my question was, is the police department ready to help handle this? I mean they wanted 2000–3000 youth a day. Masses of children probably could have been the fuel to the thing we were trying to avoid.

After the proposal was rejected, the Superintendent of Parks and Recreation sent a letter to the Chicago Initiative listing 25 reasons for why the proposal should have been funded. Even the assertive proclamation that this "was the only sports and recreation proposal that had the possibility of having significant long-range impact" (Chicago Initiative 1992g) on poor youth fell largely on deaf ears. Funders appeared more concerned about the possibility that the Initiative might inadvertently instigate the sort of violence that it was designed to prevent than about whether its summer funding might have a lasting positive impact on poor youth.

In addition to expanding summer opportunities for poor youth, the Chicago Initiative also sought to mobilize the city's resources in the event that riots actually happened. In case the proposed summer funding for youth programming did not in itself maintain peace on the streets, the Initiative's Emergency Response Coordinating Task Force would serve as a stopgap. The task force's purpose was to devise a range of strategies so that the city would be on full alert in the event of an outbreak of violence. At its first meeting on May 27, 1992, task force members identified the need for an early warning system that might detect violence before it reached the "crisis" stage. They established a hotline through which information could be dispersed between community leaders and the city, and trauma centers could be ready to respond rapidly.

The task force's role was to act as a conduit to the police about rumors of potential violence. However, law enforcement itself was left under the sole jurisdiction of the Chicago Police Department (Chicago Initiative

1992f, 1992g). The task force saw itself as playing a crucial role in mobilizing community resources to prevent the sort of violence that had occurred in Los Angeles. In this vein, a representative from the city's Department of Human Services warned:

> In the forty-five minutes it took for Los Angeles to erupt, an early warning system might have greatly altered the outcome. There was no leadership, no communication, people just let it happen. We can't let it happen here (Chicago Initiative 1993a).

ATTACKING POVERTY SYSTEMATICALLY

The sponsors of the Chicago Initiative not only sought to prevent the LA riots from snowballing to Chicago but also to address the very problem of poverty that afflicted so many U.S. cities including Chicago. Among the themes funders articulated at one of the Initiative's earliest meetings—on May 26, 1992, just three weeks after the LA riots subsided—was taking "a broad, long-term perspective on the problems," focusing on "long-term social change strategies," and viewing the Initiative as "a catalyst for *new* thinking, *new* concepts, *new* delivery mechanisms, *new* funding arrangements" (Chicago Initiative 1992k, emphasis in original). At the Chicago Initiative's official kickoff meeting on June 1st, funders created the Long-Range Planning Task Force, whose objective was to devise comprehensive strategies for reducing poverty in Chicago (Chicago Initiative 1992b). At a Distribution Committee meeting on June 11, funder called for a "change in how funders view their role in problem solving"—a focus on "root causes" (Chicago Initiative 1992n).

In a letter distributed that summer to prospective sponsors of the Chicago Initiative, the president of the Foundation Consortium, an umbrella organization of Chicago-area funders, expressed enthusiasm that the collaboration could be sustained well into the future.

> In hurriedly convening a small group of grantmakers to brainstorm philanthropy's role and interest in the Chicago Initiative, I was pleased that the funders not only recognized the need for urgent action and a mechanism that could facilitate such, but that they were also asking hard questions about the need for long-term strategies, policy-driven solutions, and sustained collaborative problem solving. This long-range planning has been incorporated into The Chicago Initiative (Chicago Initiative 1992l).

In another letter simultaneously being distributed to prospective sponsors, the Chicago Fund staff person chiefly responsible for the operation of the

Chicago Initiative described the imperative of devising a long-range agenda to address the systemic causes of urban poverty.

> All members of the Initiative realize that the proposed [summer] activities
> are stopgap measures and that the problems to be addressed in the inner
> city will persist beyond the end of this summer. A Long-Range Planning
> Task Force organized within the Initiative will study which elements of
> the summer's activities should be maintained, with what purpose, in what
> structure and for how long (Chicago Initiative 1992m).

This task force consisted entirely of community representatives and, over the course of the three-year duration of the Chicago Initiative, had anywhere from 22–78 participants. During the summer of 1992, as the Chicago Initiative was allocating grants aimed at violence prevention, the Long-Range Planning Task Force worked to formulate a plan for sustaining the Initiative into the foreseeable future and broadening its antipoverty focus. This work continued into the fall, and in December 1992 the task force issued a detailed planning report that began by stating, "We didn't need the fires in Los Angeles to tell us about our own communities. Chicago is burning with rage, violence, and despair" (Chicago Initiative 1992o:1).

The task force embraced the perspective that the violence in LA was a *rebellion*, not a riot. This semantic distinction drew upon a critical reading of the dominant framing of the violence by the news media and political and policy elites. Whereas the term "riot" identified haphazard acts of violence as the core problem that needed to be addressed, seeing the violence in LA as a "rebellion" brought to light its structural underpinnings and raised broader questions about how to tackle the deep-seated causes of poverty such as unemployment, racism, and leveled aspirations for upward mobility (Hunt 1997).

The Long-Range Planning Task Force embarked on twin goals that were common to all of the comprehensive community initiatives simultaneously taking place across American cities: to devise a systematic plan for revitalizing poor urban neighborhoods, and to effect this plan through collaboration between funders and grantees.

Neighborhood Revitalization

The Long-Range Planning Task Force, in its final planning report, grounded its work in a criticism of the piecemeal fashion in which antipoverty programs are typically carried out.

> The structure of government programs and, in some instances, foundation funding, prevents provision of services to the whole child, the whole family, the whole individual. The scramble for scarce resources forces agencies to take whatever funding is available, even if it means offering fragmented services that do not really meet people's needs. Some agencies are struggling to offer the kinds of comprehensive services needed in spite of these barriers but they face enormous difficulties (Chicago Initiative 1992o:14).

The task force's final planning report particularly criticized the tendency for funders to approach antipoverty programs with "tunnel vision" by only supporting "discrete problem categories" like after-school programs and job training, rather than addressing the underlying reasons why people become poor and tend to remain poor (Chicago Initiative 1992o:4).

People involved in the long-range planning for other comprehensive community initiatives voiced similar criticisms. Jim Rause, cofounder of the Enterprise Foundation, the major sponsor of the Sandtown-Winchester Neighborhood Transformation Initiative in Baltimore, believed that poverty-related problems like drugs, crime, indecent housing, and joblessness must be addressed as a whole given that these problems are "cancers that eat into our economic health, raise the cost of government, and impair our labor force. They are a serious threat to our well-being as a nation" (quoted in Brown, Butler, and Hamilton 2001:3).

As an alternative to the fragmented approaches foundations typically take in addressing poverty, the Chicago Initiative's Long-Range Planning Task Force advocated a comprehensive vision for neighborhood revitalization, which involved the linking of family, economic, and community development. Family development involved integrating the provision of basic social services concerning nutrition, mental health, after-school programs, childcare, and job training. Economic development focused on creating jobs, bolstering manufacturing, improving access to credit, and promoting entrepreneurship. Community development aimed to make neighborhoods safer and healthier for children and families and to increase people's faith in the ties that bound them to one another (Stagner and Duran 1997).

This vision for revitalizing poor neighborhoods was shared across comprehensive community initiatives. Consider, for example, how a report issued by the Annie E. Casey Foundation described the foundation's sponsorship of the Rebuilding Communities Initiative, which targeted a specific poor neighborhood in each of the following cities—Boston, Philadelphia, Washington, D.C., Denver, and Detroit:

Children who live in distressed urban neighborhoods—places with high rates of crime and violence, severe unemployment, widespread poverty, poor housing, and weakened systems of family and social support—face tremendous risks and disadvantages that can only be overcome by the most resilient and fortunate among them. Recognizing that the neighborhood environments in which children live profoundly affect their life prospects, the Annie E. Casey Foundation launched a new initiative in 1993 to help transform troubled neighborhoods into safe and supportive environments for children and their families (Burns and Spilka 1997:1).

In an interview, a member of the Chicago Initiative's Long-Range Planning Task Force described the rationale for revitalizing poor neighborhoods by integrating family, economic, and community development.

We couldn't create jobs without also making sure that people who live in the communities had the skills and capacities to use the jobs. Otherwise, the jobs would go to somebody else. If you improve the community but don't really have people who know how to live in the community and be part of it, they'll get bumped out to people who can pay the rents and have a more improved community. If you improve skills but the community is unsafe and there aren't jobs, people leave.

In a separate interview, another member of the Long-Range Planning Task Force further elaborated:

The vision that I came away with is that you cannot do one thing without doing all three. You can't go into a community and if you, I mean, if you look at Grand Boulevard [a poor neighborhood on the South Side of Chicago], how much money have we funded to that community in service delivery? It's not any stronger, any better, any more capable in my opinion than it was before. Because all they're looking at is service delivery. And, no matter what they say—they're "empowering" people—they aren't. All they're doing is giving all of the services that need to be delivered. So, you've got a couple of isolated incidents of some economic development, but it's got to integrate together.

Collaboration between Funders and Grantees

In carrying out their plans to revitalize low-income neighborhoods, comprehensive community initiatives strived to foster collaborative relationships among an array of entities that work on poverty-related issues yet do not normally come together to formulate antipoverty programs. This group included community-based organizations, foundations, school boards, police departments, local businesses, and government agencies. The key relationship that deserves attention and scrutiny was collaboration between funders and grantees.

The grandiose significance that foundations attached to collaborating with grantees can be seen by looking closely at the rhetoric funders espoused about collaboration.[4] For example, in its final planning report the Chicago Initiative's Long-Range Planning Task stated that collaboration was essential to achieving its goal of revitalizing low-income neighborhoods.

> To reconnect disenfranchised families and individuals with economic opportunity, the communities they live in must serve a useful purpose in the larger economy and offer a living environment which is hospitable and nurturing. Community organizations, religious institutions, CDCs (community development corporations), service providers, businesses, schools and colleges must come together to form the community's "inner circle." These local organizations and institutions must collaborate to create a common vision for the future of these communities (Chicago Initiative 1992o:8).

The Annie E. Casey Foundation further elaborated why empowering community leaders was critical to comprehensive community initiatives' success in revitalizing low-income neighborhoods.

> Each neighborhood's vision of the future is best created by those who have the biggest stake in it—community residents, and representatives from other important local organizations, agencies and businesses. Such a bottom-up plan is more likely to represent real needs and interests and therefore has a better chance of being implemented. Further, the Foundation's approach [seeks] to empower people through participation in the planning processes, and then through involvement in local governance structures which would continue to monitor and guide plan implementation. Such participation [will] in time create the new leadership and local power needed to continue championing community interests (Burns and Spilka 1997:17).

The impetus for the sponsors of comprehensive community initiatives to collaborate with community-based organizations grew out of an interest among foundations in funding collaborations among grantees. This practice entailed giving a grant to a cluster of nonprofits to work together by integrating their different piecemeal reform strategies into a holistic problem-solving agenda. It is no coincidence that foundations' interest in collaboration among nonprofits burgeoned at the same time that comprehensive community initiatives were experiencing their greatest growth; indeed, these initiatives played a crucial role in institutionalizing grantee collaborations within American philanthropy.

A telling indicator of this trend can be seen in Table 5, which indicates the results of an online search, via *Literature of the Nonprofit Sector* on the Foundation Center's Homepage (http://fdncenter.org), for articles that contain the word "collaboration" for the years 1976–2000. This search engine is perhaps the most thorough means available to access published material on philanthropy. Through 1991, there was never more than one article about collaboration, and for several years there were zero. In 1992, there were two citations and then the number began to climb steadily, reaching a peak of 29 in 1994, 1999, and 2000.

Table 5: Results of Search for Articles with the Word "Collaboration" via
Literature of the Nonprofit Sector on the Foundation Center's Homepage

Year	Number of citations	Year	Number of citations
1976	0	1989	0
1977	0	1990	1
1978	0	1991	0
1979	0	1992	2
1980	1	1993	8
1981	0	1994	29
1982	0	1995	18
1983	0	1996	12
1984	1	1997	13
1985	1	1998	22
1986	0	1999	29
1987	0	2000	29
1988	0		

These data concur with an Urban Institute study that surveyed 1,192 foundations. Sixty-nine percent reported that they sought to fund collaboration among their grantees, and 42 percent of this group indicated that they stipulated collaboration as a requirement for receiving funding (Ostrower 2005). In this regard, it is telling that one of the community leaders I interviewed indicated that he heard the word "collaboration" uttered literally thousands of times during a three-day conference he attended in 1994 about community and economic development. He counted one particular speaker using the term thirty-seven times!

During the early nineties a cottage industry consisting of conferences, workshops, books, and training sessions was emerging around the country regarding collaboration among grantees. These information outlets aimed to educate prospective collaborators about how to work through their differences and embrace a holistic approach to urban problems, particularly poverty. One such forum that I learned about during the course of my Chicago Initiative research was Collaborative Ventures, which Madison Trust sponsored in conjunction with the Foundation Consortium from April 1993 through March 1994. In an interview, the president of the Foundation Consortium commented on this project's institutional roots and goals:

> Because the field [of philanthropy] was talking about collaborative funding and because foundations were talking more and more about the need for nonprofits to work more collaboratively—and in fact nonprofits were recognizing perhaps some benefits of partnering and collaborating—Madison decided to fund some work that we co-sponsored that would analyze collaborative work around the city to try to tease out what really was collaboration.

Collaborative Ventures brought local nonprofits together to learn from one another about the process of collaboration, and in so doing, to develop a general model of how it worked. The goal was to identify and work through the many obstacles that stood in the way of successful collaboration, as a means toward engendering more effective collaborations in the future (Chicago Initiative 1993b).

BUYING PRESTIGE

On top of the explicit reasons that funders stated for supporting comprehensive community initiatives, there was an added organizational benefit of sponsorship that they left unsaid. Funders sought to gain prestige for creating these initiatives, and particularly for the timing and manner in which they did so. A group acquires prestige by enacting public performances that elicit the respect and deference of another group. Prestige cannot be acquired unilaterally but rather requires a transaction between the group seeking it and the group conferring it (Scott 1989).

The illustration at hand involves how comprehensive community initiatives were steeped in elaborate rhetoric aimed to bolster the organizational prestige of their sponsors. This rhetoric aimed to impress upon grantees that funders were accountable for ameliorating the problems facing poor neighborhoods. Through their sponsorship, funders created two kinds of glowing images: that they were acting socially responsible in the wake of a crisis and that they were eliciting the unprecedented participation of the poor in their own problem solving. In fostering these images, funders sought to attain a kind of prestige that is unique to philanthropy: prestige that can literally be bought through the allocation of grants (Galaskiewicz 1985).

Acting Socially Responsible in the Wake of a Crisis

Whether the sponsors of comprehensive community initiatives framed the precipitating call for action as the LA riots or as the myriad problems associated with concentrated urban poverty, they stood to look good for taking socially responsible action amidst what they regarded as an urban "crisis." In the case of the Chicago Initiative, its twenty-seven sponsors seized the opportunity to impress upon community-based organizations that they were proactively attempting to prevent riots from wreaking havoc on the city.

Sponsors framed their imperative for taking action as stemming *not* principally from their own fears of riots but from a moral duty to respond to fears expressed by community leaders across the city's poor neighborhoods. Several of the funders I interviewed indicated that there was consensus among community leaders attending early organizational meetings of the Chicago Initiative that the city was particularly susceptible to violence following the LA riots. The phrase I heard repeatedly in my interviews with funders was that "to a person" there was agreement at these meetings that Chicago was susceptible to the kinds of violence that wreaked havoc on Los Angeles.

This image of a community consensus of fear is one that sponsors played up in their fundraising pitches, as indicated by the letter that the president of the Foundation Consortium distributed during the summer of 1992 to prospective sponsors of the Chicago Initiative.

> We are personally convinced that the need for the Chicago Initiative is clear. Youth-serving agencies report that tensions in the city are running

higher than usual this summer. Gang activity and violence are already up significantly (Chicago Initiative 1992l).

In their official, public framing of their actions to prevent local violence following the LA riots, sponsors strategically de-emphasized the fact that they had invited community leaders to meetings to learn what, given the recent violence in Los Angeles, their organizations were planning to do to offset a long, hot summer in Chicago. Hence, by rhetorically enrolling the residents of these neighborhoods as the engines of their goodwill efforts, sponsors staked out a basis for legitimately claiming to fulfill a social responsibility to the urban poor by addressing concerns principally identified by poor constituencies

Would there have been riots in Chicago had the Chicago Initiative not been created? Although it is impossible to know for sure, raising this question points to what is especially interesting about the Initiative's having come about when it did and how it did. How likely it was that the LA riots *actually* would have snowballed to Chicago without the Chicago Initiative is not the pertinent issue here. The key point to underscore is that sponsors of the Chicago Initiative stood to look good by making a highly visible and quite substantial commitment to the poor while the media spotlight was focused on racial violence and the plight of the urban poor. In an interview one funder candidly pointed out:

> Now, was there any indication that we were going to have those types of problems [that Los Angeles was experiencing]? Not really. But, in a major urban area there's always the potential. And that was really the impetus for getting everybody together. Did that drive the discussions and so on? Not really. I mean, there wasn't, "Gee, we need to do something or we're going to have all kinds of problems." But, it [the LA riots] was really the seed that brought everyone together at the table.

Funders, therefore, acted upon their fears of riots opportunistically. Since it was unknowable whether Chicago objectively faced a greater likelihood of violence because of the LA riots, funders stood to look good by banding together and proactively taking steps to avert a crisis. Therefore, while sponsoring the Chicago Initiative had the manifest function of addressing funders' very real fears of riots, the timing and purpose of pooling their money together had the latent function of bolstering these foundations' organizational prestige.[5]

The Chicago Initiative's Communications Task Force facilitated funders' cultivation of a prestigious image of social responsibility throughout

Chicago's poor neighborhoods. This task force publicized the various positive things that the Chicago Initiative's grants were accomplishing and placed particular emphasis on getting the word out to poor constituencies that were not "'plugged in' to mainstream media" (Chicago Initiative 1992j). The achievements highlighted by the task force included (Chicago Initiative 1992d, 1992e):

- The Chicago Initiative disbursed $2.4 million in 40 of the 77 neighborhoods officially recognized by the city of Chicago.
- In total, 1,298 new jobs were created.
- Job training programs were set up for 544 adolescents and young adults, and 129 of them got placed into jobs. Seventy-nine percent of these youth were African-American, 19 percent were Latino, and the remaining 2 percent were white or from another racial group

The Communications Task Force capitalized on the fact that the national news media was giving urban social problems unusually high attention because of the LA riots. Publicizing the summer grants enabled funders to forge an image of social responsibility regardless of whether these grants would ultimately prove to be enough to prevent riots. If there had been widespread violence that summer, then funders would have been justified in claiming that they at least did what they could to avert it. If *race* riots did not occur (as proved to be the case—the violence following the Chicago Bulls' championship victory in June was hardly racial), then funders could legitimately take some credit for preserving law and order in the city.

The fact that the Chicago Initiative's unique contribution to keeping the peace could not be objectively measured fueled funders' impetus for taking credit for proactively averting a crisis. Certainly no other authoritative voice with access to the mainstream media was about to challenge such a claim. In an interview, one funder characterized sponsors' efforts to cultivate prestige among the poor by piggybacking on the media attention given to the LA riots as a "cheap way to hedge your bets."

Funders' sense of their social responsibilities to the poor in the wake of urban crises had roots extending back to the array of elite-sponsored initiatives that came into being during the long, hot summers of the 1960s. Many corporations created urban affairs departments that disbursed money within poor minority neighborhoods. Of the 247 companies studied by Cohn (1970), 201 had such departments in place by 1970 yet only five of these programs existed before 1965. Companies also joined forces with one another to forge better rapport with the residents of poor neighborhoods, as was the case in Chicago with Concerned Corporate Leaders (a participant in the Chicago Initiative), which was founded in the wake of the 1968 riots by a group of local white businessmen.

At the federal level, the Johnson administration allocated more funds to local community action agencies following the riot that devastated the Watts section of Los Angeles in 1965. Moreover, corporations and the federal government joined forces in embracing affirmative action as a measure aimed to redirect black frustrations away from violence and toward employment opportunities (Halpern 1995; Skrentny 1996). Whether the initiatives came from foundations, corporations, the government, or some combination thereof, in each case elites saw their support of civil rights, jobs, education, and housing as a way to capture some of the spotlight created by episodes of rioting and gain prestige for appearing socially responsible toward the poor (Haines 1988).

Eliciting the Participation of the Poor in their Own Problem Solving

The second image sponsors of comprehensive community initiatives fostered that won them prestige among community-based organizations was that these initiatives empowered poor constituencies to participate in mitigating their own problems. Sponsors of the Chicago Initiative played up that it was unprecedented for funders to share power with grantees. Consider the text of a report describing the terms under which funders came together to create the Initiative.

> It was an unusual gambit to present to funders. Philanthropies and charities who guard their autonomy in decision-making were being asked to relinquish both authority and money all at once to a process that was just evolving and whose procedure for grantmaking was entirely decentralized. The task force would find appropriate agencies and solicit proposals, then sift through those requests and pass on the best—what was effective in organization and impact—to the funders, who would decide as a committee, with whatever funds could be raised (Chicago Initiative 1993a:14).

The Chicago Initiative cultivated the glowing image that its collaborative structure was distinct from traditional philanthropy, which involves a foundation unilaterally deciding the kinds of needs that merit funding within a poor neighborhood, issuing requests for proposals, and then allocating monies as it so chooses. In the unique context created by the Chicago Initiative, funders, grantees, and other parties with expertise and concern about the problems of urban poverty would be sitting around the table formulating policy together, which would consequently enable community-based organizations to gain unprecedented access to foundations' purse strings. In a summary report, a consultant to the Chicago Initiative characterized this image of democratic philanthropy that its sponsors sought to cultivate:

> The Chicago Initiative is viewed as different primarily because it has brought together a new mix of players to sit together at the table. The Chicago Initiative provided the forum for various sectors to come together, get acquainted, learn from each other, and begin working jointly toward some solutions (Suleiman, 1994).

Hence, the Chicago Initiative, like other comprehensive community initiatives, purported to define the needs of the poor—and accordingly distribute grants—through a process that was inclusive of all parties with expertise and concern about mitigating poverty (Baker, Chaskin, and Wynn 1996). The collaboration model aimed to transform the status of community-based organizations from being outsiders to policy processes traditionally shaped largely by foundations, to becoming insiders to these processes alongside their foundation partners (Taylor 2001).

This image of mutual participation among an array of actors only some of whom traditionally have a say in antipoverty reform was one that sponsors of the Chicago Initiative saw as a powerful selling point for eliciting wider sponsorship. In a letter to its foundation members aimed toward eliciting contributions to the Initiative, the director of the Foundation Consortium wrote:

> This community-wide collaborative process is unprecedented in Chicago. Perhaps it marks a new way of community problem solving. Most assuredly it challenges grantmaking institutions to rethink their traditional role and invites them to be equal partners with nonprofits, government, and other sectors in a collaborative community problem solving apparatus (Chicago Initiative 1992l).

Similarly, in a fundraising letter sent to the president of one of Chicago largest foundations, the executive director of the Chicago Fund, the foundation that spearheaded the Chicago Initiative, wrote:

> In providing its support the [Chicago Fund] has taken an action which it hardly ever takes and which contradicts a specific [Chicago Fund] policy. It has given the funds to others to grant. We have done so because of our strong belief in the immediacy of the need, our commitment to the process and our understanding that if this initiative is to

work we all have to have trust in the good will which has been generated (Chicago Initiative 1992a).

The prospect of poor people participating in the process of
antipoverty reform had deep-seated historical precedent, and consequently
carried considerable popular support. The general idea of citizen participation in problem solving tapped a longstanding belief within American culture about the significant strides that the disenfranchised could make in
improving their lives if they did not depend on aid from elites, particularly
from the government. This idea lay at the root of the settlement house
movement which during the late nineteenth and early twentieth centuries,
as we saw in Chapter Two, encouraged poor immigrants to become actively
involved in bettering their own social conditions. Citizen participation,
more recently during the 1960s, was the cornerstone of the war on
poverty's community action program, with its emphasis on the maximum
feasible participation of the poor in bettering their own social conditions
(Halpern 1995; Katz 1989; Zarefsky 1986).

In sum, the efforts made by foundations to cultivate prestige through
their sponsorship of the Chicago Initiative were significant for two reasons.
First, these efforts indicated that funders' motivations for sponsorship
extended considerably beyond what they articulated explicitly either at the
time, which is contained in the Chicago Initiative's archival record, or what
they said in the interviews I conducted with them during the year after the
collaboration disbanded. And second, funders' attempts to buy prestige
among poor constituencies created opportunities for grantees to exercise
greater influence within the Chicago Initiative. This is the subject I turn to
next, in Chapter Four.

Chapter Four
Community-based Reasons
for Getting Involved

Whereas to its sponsors the Chicago Initiative was unprecedented in that it created a funder-grantee collaboration and allocated millions of dollars in the wake of a crisis, poor constituencies had reason to question the hype that sponsors attached to their actions. The leaders of community-based organizations were cynical about the kinds of social changes that the Chicago Initiative would effect, bearing in mind the legacies left by prior elite-sponsored antipoverty initiatives. This cynicism stemmed from the view that these earlier initiatives were created amidst great fanfare, yet did not live up to their billing and instead became co-opted by their elite benefactors. It is important, therefore, to consider how community leaders channeled their cynicism into concerted efforts to get sponsors to live up to their rhetoric about sustaining the Chicago Initiative as an ongoing collaboration to revitalize low-income neighborhoods.

CYNICISM TOWARD SPONSORS

For the community leaders invited to collaborate with sponsors within the Chicago Initiative, this invitation was a mixed blessing. On the one hand, it carried the prospect of significantly expanding the funds available for antipoverty reform. On the other hand, community-based organizations were weary of entrusting foundations as partners, only to feel betrayed yet again by a paternalistic elite offering to lend a helping hand. Indeed, community-based organizations interpreted what participating in the Chicago Initiative might mean through the lenses of their collective memories of prior elite attempts to mitigate social inequalities.

The most direct focal point for community-based cynicism, particularly among African Americans, was the legacy left by the various antipoverty initiatives undertaken during the 1960s. Both at the time and with increasing frequency in retrospect, black community leaders were inclined to see government, foundation, and corporate responses to the riots that took place during the five long, hot summers of the mid-sixties as little more than self-interested attempts by white elites to address their growing fear of poor blacks. Some blacks viewed urban crisis initiatives, moreover, as a means for white policymakers to absolve themselves of long-term responsibility for revitalizing poor black communities (Trattner 1984).

Furthermore, many black community leaders felt particular resentment over the unrealized promises of the war on poverty's community action program. The Johnson administration cloaked this program in rhetoric about fostering the "maximum feasible participation" of the poor in antipoverty reforms, yet subsequently gave in to pressure by mayors to limit the amount of involvement the poor would have in proposing and implementing neighborhood reforms. Historian Robert Halpern (1995: 118–19) notes that as the war on poverty began to unravel, a sense of disillusionment and betrayal became entrenched within poor black communities:

> Inner-city residents and black Civil Rights leaders were disillusioned by the inability of any reform strategy—use of the courts, nonviolent direct action, or a federally declared War on Poverty—to compel white America to respond to their exclusion. There was a growing sense of unfulfilled promises and betrayal within the inner city. The experiences of urban renewal and community action had confirmed inner-city residents' doubts about whites rather than their hopes.

While the legacies left by the antipoverty initiatives of the 1960s were a major reason for community-based organizations to question sponsors' heralding of the Chicago Initiative, this cynicism extended considerably further back in time. Given the racial differences between the sponsors and community-based organizations involved in the Chicago Initiative (the former being overwhelmingly white, the latter overwhelmingly black), community-based organizations' skeptical posture can be traced as far back as the history of white-black race relations in the U.S.

Skepticism among poor black constituencies toward the motives behind white social reform emerged and became reinforced over the long history of racial antagonism dating back to the slave period, and in particular to the mistrust that developed around the efforts of charitable whites. During slavery, some whites felt that blacks would live better if they returned to Africa. Yet, even those blacks favoring emigration were suspicious of white efforts to underwrite their transportation costs. Years after emancipation, these suspicions remained. Around the turn of the 20th century, there was impassioned debate between Booker T. Washington, the most prominent black leader of his day, and W.E.B. Du Bois, his most outspoken critic. Washington believed that blacks needed white assistance in order to advance in a white-dominated society, and he appealed to famed industrialist Andrew Carnegie in 1903 for $600,000 to offer blacks access to industrial education at the Tuskegee Institute in Alabama. Du Bois criticized Washington for not advocating that blacks instead organize to resist Jim Crow legislation. Du Bois viewed white support for black industrial education as an attempt to co-opt the aspirations of blacks by making them content with laboring for white capitalists. Du Bois believed that this co-optation would prevent blacks from recognizing the advantages of obtaining greater access to higher education (Broderick 1962; Du Bois 1962; Green and Bailey 1997; Washington 1962).

It is through these historical lenses that community-based organizations assessed whether or not the Chicago Initiative was likely to produce meaningful antipoverty reforms. In an interview, an African-American community activist spoke about poor constituencies' inclination to see the Chicago Initiative as just another dressed up elite response to urban crisis:

> There are many people who were part of the planning for the Chicago Initiative who remembered when rioting actually took place and wondered that you can still go through certain West-Side communities and see neighborhoods exactly as they existed when the fires went out. There wasn't any civic interest. There are communities in Lawndale, in Austin—Lawndale particularly comes to mind for me. The response at that time was, "if these are the neighborhoods they live in, so let them burn them down. They can live with this." And from '68 until the Reginald Denny thing [the LA riots], there are some neighborhoods that hadn't seen any more interest from the civic, philanthropic, or public community than that. So it was curious, particularly I think to the West-Side contingents, that the thought that something that recently happened in LA might happen in Chicago and therefore we ought to maybe throw a little money at preventing it—well then, it did happen here and they'd done nothing about it.

In a separate interview, another black community activist, who had been involved in the war on poverty during the 1960s, expressed similar reservations about the Chicago Initiative:

I'm cynical because unless there is a crisis, dollars don't float. I'm part of the Model Cities cadre of people who worked in that effort—Job Corps effort and the Great Society plans and all that kind of stuff. They all developed around crises.

EMBRACING THE SUMMER GRANTS CAMPAIGN

A small number of community-based organizations refused to participate in the Chicago Initiative because, as one African American community activist put it when I interviewed him, these groups did not fear riots but that funders might give them false hopes only to exploit them yet again. I am unsure precisely how many organizations of this kind there were because when I asked this man and other activists if they knew of particular non-participants whom I might speak with, the response was consistently no. They were unwilling to refer me to interview these non-participants since these people might be suspicious of why I wanted to interview them, presuming that, as a white academic researcher, I had allegiances to foundations and might therefore be yet another source of exploitation.

Despite the deep-seated community-based cynicism toward foundations' motives, relatively few community leaders balked at the chance to participate in the Chicago Initiative. Even though many community leaders questioned whether sponsors would sustain their commitments, most of these community leaders converted their skepticism into action by joining the collaboration and, as we shall see later in this chapter, some of them worked arduously to try to transform the Chicago Initiative into the unprecedented and ongoing antipoverty initiative that its sponsors claimed it would become.

In order to understand why so many community-based organizations embraced the Chicago Initiative's summer grants campaign, we need to form a picture of what these organizations shared in common. All of them carried out antipoverty programs in low-income communities of color across Chicago. These organizations were either nonprofit organizations or organizations that did not yet have the necessary legal 501(c)(3) status to apply for grants. The members of this latter group sought funding under the jurisdiction of another community-based organization that served as its fiscal agent. In either case, these organizations depended heavily on foundations to meet their programming goals.

The need for funds is a chronic concern for community-based organizations, whose budgets are lean and whose staff work arduously to raise whatever moneys they can. This is the case regardless of whether these organizations are relatively new or well established. A woman who coordinated the Chicago Initiative's summer grantmaking campaign commented in an interview that for this reason most community-based organizations could not have conceived passing up the opportunity to participate in the Chicago Initiative.

> When you're in a community that's really in need of summer activities for their youth, you don't just say "No, I don't want to be bothered by this organization, because I don't know if I'm going to get funding next year." The need is immediate and present at that point and you're happy to get the money.

Funding concerns were particularly dire for community-based organizations during the early 1990s, making the Chicago Initiative an especially welcomed new source of money. For several years, the budget for the Job Training Partnership Act, the main federal revenue that cities received for summer youth employment, had been annually cut. A member of the Chicago Initiative's Jobs/Job Training Task Force who kept track of these trends reported in an interview that in 1981 Chicago had $40 million for summer employment but by the summer of 1996, that amount had fallen to approximately $12 million. These cuts meant that while in 1980 Chicago enrolled 43,000 poor youth in an 8-week summer employment program, by 1992 there was only enough money for 12,000 six-week jobs (Chicago Initiative 1993a).

Even though President George Bush had taken decisive action immediately after the LA riots that appeared to offset these funding cuts, the new aid that he made available to cities across the country was allocated according to unemployment rather than poverty rates. Hence, this aid did not go to the growing number of working poor who, despite being part of the paid labor force, still faced chronic difficulties making ends meet. Given the funding cuts and constraints that grantees were at the time experiencing, in the words of the coordinator of the Chicago Initiative's summer programs "people were hungry" for the money that the collaboration had made available.

This hunger translated into community-based organizations telling sponsors what they wanted to hear. Recall from Chapter Three that a key part of funders' claims to be taking socially responsible action in the wake of the LA riots was their framing the summer grants as a response *not* to their own fears of riots but to fears expressed by community leaders across the city's poor neighborhoods. While community leaders did indeed express these fears, we must bear in mind that their doing so was part of the "public transcript" between funders and community-based organizations. This term, which I am borrowing from Scott (1990), characterizes the asymmetrical dialogue that took place between these groups; a dialogue in which community-based organizations were politically invested in speaking, and more generally behaving, in ways that validated funders' own sense of the legitimacy of their actions and of themselves.

Indeed, community leaders were keenly aware that by confirming funders' sense that they were proactively addressing community-based fears of riots, this would likely contribute to funders putting more money on the table that summer. Community leaders came to early meetings of the Chicago Initiative with full knowledge that how they comported themselves in response to sponsors' queries about the prospects of impending violence could have a direct bearing on the availability of funds that summer for youth programs. It is noteworthy that in the weeks following the LA riots funders invited community representatives to meetings and asked them to explain "what they planned to do to offset a long, hot summer in Chicago." Given their organizations' financial needs, it comes as no surprise that these representatives publicly affirmed funders' fears that tensions were especially high in Chicago's poor neighborhoods following the riots.

A community leader, who eventually became executive director of the Chicago Initiative, characterized community leaders' posture toward funders within the public transcript:

> I'm telling you that when you put something like that [increased funding] out there, if I'm a nonprofit lookin' for some money, you think I ain't gonna play into that? Let's get real! Hell yeah! They gettin' ready to tear up, y'all better do somethin'! Okay? I mean, give me a break. These executive agency directors are intelligent and if there is a perception among the folks that control the money and the power that somethin' [violent] is gonna happen unless you move, am I, as a community representative, not gonna feed into that?

Contrast the above statement with the recurring indication I got in my interviews with community activists that, within the "hidden transcript" (Scott 1990) that these activists shared among themselves when outside the presence of funders, there were in truth few elevated fears of local violence following the LA riots. In an interview, one community leader commented:

> [The Chicago Initiative] felt from the outset like something which was paying lip service to an idea that wasn't supported by any of the service community. Documentation that there was likely to be urban violence, it was all anecdotal.

Another community leader summed up the ambivalent stance that drove so many community-based organizations to participate in the Initiative's summer grants campaign by commenting: "The real response among service providers was that [the Initiative] was a flawed notion but it's a resource of money, so let's apply for it."

Those community-based organizations that participated in the summer grants campaign were of three types. First, there were *grassroots organizations*, which often occupied offices no bigger or savvier than a basement and survived precariously from day to day on shoestring budgets. Though they were the most suspicious participants of funders' motives, they served on programming task forces and applied for grant money chiefly because they saw the Initiative as offering them a chance to become known by mainstream foundations. None of these organizations received a summer grant in 1992.

Next, there were *neighborhood agencies*, which were located in a particular neighborhood outside of downtown Chicago and provided services within that geographic area. They differed from grassroots organizations in that they already had some networks with mainstream funders, and thus saw the Initiative as a likely source of much-needed continued support. They were cynical about sponsors' motives but pragmatically aware of the financial benefits of getting a piece of the pie. Each of them received one grant in 1992.

Finally, there were *downtown agencies*, which were the least cynical about funders' motives. These agencies, which were based in or near downtown Chicago and provided social services throughout the city, simply accepted as a given that funders routinely put their own interests ahead of the poor communities that they supported. In embracing the view that philanthropic money is never wholly "clean" but yet is money nonetheless, these agencies did not concern themselves too much with the moral implications of being at the table alongside funders. Instead, downtown agencies pragmatically viewed getting involved in the Initiative as a way to secure a new source of needed revenues for the summer. And, they were in the best position to secure such funding since they were already well networked with funders. The strength of downtown agencies' prior network ties to funders is illustrated by the fact that, although only six of these agencies received summer grants from the Chicago Initiative in 1992, these six collectively amassed 33.6 percent of the $2.4 million allocated that summer.

TACTICALLY CONFERRING PRESTIGE ON FUNDERS

The financial motivation of those community activists who comprised the Chicago Initiative's Long-Range Planning Task Force was not money for summer youth programs but ongoing funding for a comprehensive program to revitalize the city's low-income neighborhoods. Despite the pent-up resentment that existed inside poor neighborhoods concerning prior efforts by elites to mitigate poverty, the community activists who served on this task force saw the Chicago Initiative as offering a reason for new hopes. Since the collaboration fostered opportunities for unprecedented community involvement in foundation grantmaking, one task force member described this collaboration as having "the most potential for making comprehensive change than anything I have seen in twenty years because of its multi-sector nature" (Chicago Initiative 1995a).

Although those on the Long-Range Planning Task Force were skeptical about how genuinely committed sponsors were to effecting neighborhood revitalization, these community activists viewed sponsors' escalating interest in violence prevention following the LA riots as creating a vehicle for transforming the existing paradigm concerning philanthropic responses to poverty. In other words, the Long-Range Planning Task Force sought to appropriate the Chicago Initiative's grantmaking agenda by making funders' actions resonant with their identity claims.

The community leaders who served on the Long-Range Planning Task Force sensed that although the extent of funders' genuine interest in supporting an ongoing collaboration aimed to revitalize poor communities was questionable, funders' efforts to attain prestige from displaying interest in such a possibility placed them in a liminal position susceptible to manipulation. These community leaders recognized that funders were caught between acting in ways that served to elevate their prestige, and putting their money where their mouths were. The task force's work, therefore, was implicitly grounded in the view that funders' betwixt-and-between status (Turner 1967) opened up an opportunity for enticing funders to sustain antipoverty work that they would not have otherwise considered supporting.

In an effort to wield influence within the Chicago Initiative, the community activists on the Long-Range Planning Task Force sought to validate sponsors' glowing self-image as "socially responsible" for having created this collaboration in the wake of a crisis. These community activists saw sponsors' efforts to cultivate this image around their largesse as opening up an opportunity to tactically call forth their support for comprehensive antipoverty reform. These community activists sought to strategically legitimize sponsors' portrayal of themselves as socially responsible as a means toward cementing sponsors' commitment to their stated interest in broadening the goal of the Chicago Initiative from summer violence prevention to neighborhood revitalization. In this way, these community activists behaved in a manner akin to other subordinate groups vying to manipulate elites' presentations of self for their own political gain (Scott 1990).

The Long-Range Planning Task Force simultaneously made two types of strategic legitimacy claims, each of which was aimed to resonate with funders and elicit their support. *Internal legitimacy claims* aimed to project neighborhood revitalization grants as consonant with other foundation goals. *External legitimacy claims* attempted to attach the prospect of foundations investing in neighborhood revitalization to a growing national trend toward the privatization of antipoverty reform.

Internal Legitimacy Claims

Since a focus on summer programs for poor youth had been what galvanized sponsors' interest in the Chicago Initiative following the LA riots, the Long-Range Planning Task Force sought to legitimize neighborhood revitalization by packaging its work as consistent with these programs. The task force strived to show sponsors that the goals of its neighborhood revitalization strategy were an extension of the goals of the summer youth programs.

Ironically, the Long-Range Planning Task Force embraced sponsors' discourse about helping poor youth by attacking the Chicago Initiative's summer violence prevention grants for their "Band-Aid" focus. Consider that a report issued in January 1993 concerning the feasibility of the Initiative's having a second summer of grantmaking stated that one of the ongoing goals of the Initiative would be "to make the summer component an expanded and complementary extension of the new paradigm of the Long-Range Planning Committee of the Chicago Initiative" (Chicago Initiative 1993c). That summer, the Initiative publicized that it simultaneously had short-term, intermediate, and long-term goals, but that "the long-range vision [was] at the heart of TCI and future efforts [would] reflect this" (Chicago Initiative 1993d). (I discuss the planning and implementation of the 1993 summer grants campaign in Chapter Five.)

During the fall of 1993, while plans for implementing the neighborhood revitalization agenda still remained in the early stages of development, the Long-Range Planning Task Force touted the positive impacts on poor youth of the 1993 summer violence prevention grants. The Chicago Initiative's November 1993 newsletter devoted most of its focus to "Summer Program Highlights." One column praised the grants that enabled youth to participate in midnight basketball programs. In another section, the Initiative's executive director wrote:

> With reduced government funding of programs for teens this summer,
> it is clear that many opportunities would have been unavailable to
> young people without the Chicago Initiative (Chicago Initiative 1993e).

The Chicago Initiative consequently embarked on a strategic planning process that lasted from November 1993 until February 1994. This process was fundamentally about how to incorporate the poor youth focus into the Initiative's primary mission "to support strategies in low-income communities that effectively link family, community, and economic development" (Chicago Initiative 1994a). Although the powerful rhetorical meaning of "youth" as a springboard for fundraising was not explicitly stated, it was no mere coincidence that the Initiative spent three months figuring out how to incorporate into its new mission this population that held such sway with funders.

The Long-Range Planning Task Force was aware that its fundraising efforts contained a paradox. That is, the viability of the neighborhood revitalization agenda depended on how well the task force could frame its work as intertwined with concerns about poor youth, which were the very concerns that galvanized sponsors to create the 1992 summer grants campaign. Yet, the community activists on this task force hardly saw embracing youth rhetoric as a form of capitulation to funders' grantmaking interests. Quite to the contrary, they viewed this rhetoric as offering them the ammunition they needed to critique sponsors' short-term conception of the Chicago Initiative, and to re-direct its goals instead around neighborhood revitalization.

Therefore, the Long-Range Planning Task Force embraced the youth focus strategically. It sought to hold sponsors accountable to claims they had made about how the Chicago Initiative would differ from prior philanthropic efforts mounted in the wake of a crisis. The task force viewed sponsors' projected image that the Initiative would be a "proactive, long-term collaboration" as offering ammunition for challenging their ideological bent toward short-term grants.

However, the Long-Range Planning Task Force faced a hurdle. While sponsors were attracted to summer violence prevention grants because these short-term reforms easily produced indicators of success, sustaining a collaboration to rebuild poor communities was unlikely to yield similar short-term results. Speaking about how to surmount this hurdle, a consultant to the Long-Range Planning Task Force recommended:

> I think it would be worthwhile for the Chicago Initiative to clearly articulate a vision of the quality of life expected in Chicago and its neighborhoods after many (say, twenty) years of intervention, with annual and five-year measures, along specific dimensions such as housing, jobs, health, and so on (Chicago Initiative 1993f).

The Long-Range Planning Task Force embraced this recommendation in its framing of the need to retain a short-term youth agenda as the Chicago Initiative pushed forward with plans for comprehensive neighborhood revitalization:

> The key question is how to integrate the summer activities into a long-range mission as identified by the Strategic Planning Committee. The Chicago Initiative needs to be able to point to some *immediate, short-term successes*. We need to retain some short-term program activity so that there are *deliverables* to low-income communities and evidence of progress for other TCI partners while awaiting the deliverables from the long-term agenda (Chicago Initiative 1994b, my emphasis).

The Long-Range Planning Task Force recognized that the only conceivable way to elicit sponsors' financial support for an agenda that would not quickly produce indicators of success would be to highlight enough successes for sponsors to see reason to stay involved in the planning process. The task force, therefore, sought to project the new mission statement crafted during the strategic planning process as a continuation of, rather than a departure from, the Initiative's earlier work. The Strategic Planning Committee had initially considered three future scenarios for the collaboration: 1) Close the Initiative, 2) Continue as is, or 3) Create a long-term mission. The task force obviously wanted to avoid the first option. Moreover, given that the Chicago Initiative's fundraising declined 46 percent (from $2.7 million to $1.4 million) between its first and second summers, the Long-Range Planning Task Force saw this option as becoming an imminent reality if the Initiative took the second path. Since sponsors might construe the third course of action as too much of a departure from the short-term goals that originally brought them to the table, the Long-Range Planning Task Force sought to embark on this path tactically.

In doing so, the task force played a new fundraising card by embracing the concept of "youth development," which had become a buzz term throughout the philanthropic world during the early 1990s. The term derived from social-psychological research addressing the cognitive and emotional needs of youth. The basic grantmaking goal that incorporated this concept was to support the systemic development of these needs instead of taking Band-Aid approaches to the problems of youth. Youth development seamlessly fused the Long-Range Planning Task Force's core idea of linked development with a substantive focus on poor youth, a target population that carried considerable rhetorical weight with funders.

The Long-Range Planning Task Force's credibility in embracing youth development was heightened by the fact that the Chicago Initiative was clinging to the coattails of Chicago Mayor Richard M. Daley's own initiative on behalf of poor youth. The mayor's actions were fueled by the tragic news of October 13, 1992. On that day Dantrell Davis, a seven year-old African-American boy, was killed by gang gunfire outside his home in the Cabrini-Green public housing development while on his way to school (Nickerson 1992). Like the riots in Los Angeles nearly six months earlier, though on a smaller scale, Chicago's municipal elite viewed this violence as pointing to a "crisis" that demanded responsive action. The mayor, along with the president of Madison Trust, one of the city's largest foundations, proceeded to create a task force on youth development. Instead of doing something that only targeted violence at Cabrini-Green, the task force sought to focus more generally on youth living in public housing and in other poor communities (Chicago Initiative 1993g). For nearly a year, the task force studied the problem of youth violence and in June 1994 announced "Youth Works," its recommendation to create ten after-school activity centers for youth in four of the city's poorest communities (Chicago Initiative 1994c).

In an attempt to capitalize on the fervor surrounding youth development, the Chicago Initiative formed its own Youth Development Task Force. This task force consolidated the programming task forces that had evaluated grant proposals during the 1992 and 1993 summer, violence-prevention campaigns (Chicago Initiative 1994d). There was a considerable overlap between the people who served on the mayor's task force and those who participated in the Chicago Initiative (Chicago Initiative 1994e).

At this point, the Long-Range Planning Task Force sought to re-cast the Chicago Initiative's summer accomplishments so that sponsors would see youth development and neighborhood revitalization as mutually intertwined agendas. Consequently, a discussion document distributed in June 1994 stated that "youth development strategies should be viewed as an integral component of the specific agendas of community building initiatives" (Chicago Initiative 1994f). The hope was that sponsors would deem it important to support another summer grantmaking campaign in 1994 since this time around the summer grants would be encased within a new conception of crisis. Unlike previously, this time it would be the image of an ongoing youth crisis in which even innocent kids walking to school, such as seven year-old Dantrell Davis, were in danger of being subjected to violence (Chicago Initiative 1994g). The Chicago Initiative's executive director consequently framed the neighborhood revitalization agenda as if it were an accessory to youth development, even though this agenda was the Long-Range Planning Task Force's central concern. This tactical move was evidenced by the dollar distribution within the 1995 budget she proposed for the Initiative—$2 million for youth development, compared to just $500,000 for neighborhood revitalization (Chicago Initiative 1994h).

The task force's objective was to package its neighborhood revitalization agenda as resonant with other antipoverty work being done under the guise of "youth development." In doing so, the task force highlighted what was distinct about its linked development grantmaking plan. First, it was tying youth development to the rebuilding of poor communities. In this regard, at a meeting of the Chicago Initiative's Steering Committee, one committee member commented:

> It is extremely important to articulate the funding for youth as a piece of the long-term mission for TCI. This must be understood as poverty alleviation of which youth is a special, targeted population (Chicago Initiative 1994h).

Second, the Initiative was involving youth as leaders in program planning and decision making (Chicago Initiative 1994i). Third, one of the three programming components of youth development, the creation of a youth service corps, would focus on a younger population (12–16 year olds) than existing youth development programs typically did (Chicago Initiative 1994j). And fourth, virtually all (90%) of the Initiative's funding would support programs rather than underwrite overhead costs (Chicago Initiative 1995b).

The central mechanism for community leaders' internal legitimacy claims was to appropriate language that sponsors used to justify their support of the violence prevention agenda. This language in part was about awarding grants that yielded immediate and tangible indicators of success. Since this was language that carried currency with funders, the Long-Range Planning Task Force's goal was to draw on this language in packaging the neighborhood revitalization agenda as having an affinity with the violence prevention agenda. Community leaders strategized that by framing neighborhood revitalization with rhetoric that resonated deeply with funders, they could galvanize support for this agenda.

External Legitimacy Claims

In attempting to legitimize its neighborhood revitalization agenda as worthy of financial backing, the Long-Range Planning Task Force also sought to frame this agenda as resonant with a growing national trend toward the privatization of antipoverty policy. As we saw in Chapter Two, this trend was well in place at the time that the Chicago Initiative came into being during the early nineties. Two Republican presidential administrations had spent twelve years divesting the federal government of responsibility for antipoverty policy and other types of social reform, and in the wake of this sea change a number of privately and locally supported comprehensive community initiatives came into existence.

The Long-Range Planning Task Force became particularly interested in the comprehensive community initiative in Atlanta led by former President Jimmy Carter. One of the underlying, although rarely articulated, goals of *The Atlanta Project* was to make a measurable reduction in the city's poverty rate in time for the 1996 Summer Olympics. In late March 1993, twelve people representing the Chicago Initiative took a three-day trip to Atlanta to gather information intended to help them learn how to move forward with the Initiative's neighborhood revitalization agenda. This delegation, which consisted of sponsors, members of the Long-Range Planning Task Force, and several other leading figures in the Initiative, saw the Atlanta Project as a potential model for how to do comprehensive antipoverty reform in Chicago (Chicago Initiative 1993f).

The delegation returned quite impressed that Jimmy Carter's charismatic leadership of the Atlanta Project was galvanizing strong corporate backing, which the Long-Range Planning Task Force recognized as essential if the Chicago Initiative were to endure with a neighborhood revitalization focus. However, the delegation did not like the fact that neighborhood constituencies and other religious and nonprofit leaders were being underrepresented within the Atlanta collaboration (Chicago Initiative 1993f). In an interview, one member of the Long-Range Planning Task Force claimed:

> I thought it was pretty top-down, pretty worried about how it looked out there. They've spent an awful lot of their money promoting themselves, without much really being spent in the communities. So, it seemed to us to be a lot of slick PR without a lot of substance to it.

Although the delegation viewed the Atlanta Project as a mixed bag in terms of how it was attempting to alleviate poverty in the city, members of the Long-Range Planning Task Force who went on the trip returned with a sense of optimism that the Chicago Initiative collaboration could be sustained. In particular, they were pleased by the strong interest expressed in Atlanta for developing a national community-building initiative, which would sponsor similar poverty reduction efforts in other cities across the country. More generally, task force members felt that during the trip they gathered information that could give even the most skeptical sponsors concrete examples to show that an antipoverty collaboration could be sustained in Chicago (Chicago Initiative 1993f).

The task force's optimism that it could obtain sponsorship for its neighborhood revitalization agenda heightened a few weeks after the Atlanta trip when on May 3, 1993 President Clinton announced the creation of ten federally funded "Empowerment Zones" and 100 "Enterprise Communities"—a set of proposals that became codified in the Economic Empowerment Act of 1993. This legislation bolstered the credibility of the Long-Range Planning Task Force's vision for a private and local antipoverty collaboration in Chicago, since the legislation was aimed to reduce government involvement in the revitalization of poor communities by instead giving:

> . . . local communities the incentives, deregulation and flexibility they need to work with the private sector to develop comprehensive economic strategies to generate business, create jobs, make their streets safe, and empower people to get ahead (Chicago Initiative 1993h).

The demarcated areas under this policy were to be concentrated in cities, with a smaller proportion in rural areas and on Indian reservations. All of the areas would be eligible for tax incentives as well as given special priority for federal education reform and community policing programs. Empowerment Zones qualified for additional tax incentives and could apply for funding for community and economic development (Chicago Initiative 1993h). On December 21, 1994 Chicago was designated as one of six cities for Empowerment Zone funding. Neighborhoods in three non-contiguous areas of the city's South and West sides were eligible to apply for grants.

At the time that I conducted the interviews for this book in 1996, many of those who had served on the Long-Range Planning Task Force felt that the Empowerment Zones/Enterprise Communities legislation was not living up to its hype. However, at the time that this policy was first announced in May 1993, it significantly contributed to task force members' impression that the national community-building initiative envisioned under the Atlanta Project might indeed be coming to fruition. The excitement that the Clinton administration generated on the national level fueled the Long-Range Planning Task Force's growing belief that there was sufficient external justification for sponsors to want to support the Chicago Initiative's neighborhood revitalization agenda.

Indeed, at a meeting in January 1994, the chair of the Long-Range Planning Task Force saw the Chicago Initiative as having an unprecedented opportunity to take:

. . . advantage of the "convergence of agendas" in trying to find new
solutions to urban poverty. For example, the Clinton Administration,
through the Empowerment Zones legislation, is recommending the TCI
model as a key component of cities' applications for funding to this
program. We are uniquely positioned to take advantage of this window
of opportunity because of the work we have been doing for the past
one and one-half years through the Long-Range Planning Task Force
(Chicago Initiative 1994b).

In a letter to a foundation requesting money to underwrite the costs of the
strategic planning process surrounding the implementation of the neighborhood revitalization agenda, the executive director of the Chicago Initiative
claimed:

What is happening through the Chicago Initiative represents a national
trend of community residents and non-profits that are coming together
to reclaim and rebuild very poor communities. However, there are three
key elements of our project that place us in the forefront of these
national urban community-building initiatives. First is the number and
range of individuals from diverse sectors of the city who have been willing to contribute countless hours of volunteer time to make the Initiative a reality. Second is our comprehensive approach to community
planning and revitalization and, finally, our intent to broker technical
assistance and other resources for both new and established collaborative planning efforts (Chicago Initiative 1993i).

Of these three claimed measures of distinction behind the Chicago Initiative's neighborhood revitalization agenda, the Long-Range Planning Task
Force emphasized the second one the most. The notion here was that while
other comprehensive community initiatives were concentrating on a particular neighborhood or section of a city, the Chicago Initiative was focusing
on *all* of Chicago (Chicago Initiative 1995c). The Long-Range Planning
Task Force was quite aware that sponsors might be inclined to view supporting the neighborhood revitalization agenda as superfluous with the federal Empowerment Zone funding being given to Chicago. Therefore, the
task force emphasized that its work was especially in need of support in the
many poor sections of the city that had not been included under the Clinton proposal (Chicago Initiative 1995d).

DISPLACING CYNICISM WITH STRATEGIC ACTION

The Long-Range Planning Task Force worked arduously to position its neighborhood revitalization agenda as sufficiently attractive so that sponsors of the Chicago Initiative would be interested in sustaining the collaboration on an ongoing basis well past the distribution of "emergency" summer grants that propelled the creation of this collaboration in the first place. When looking at this task force's work within the broader context of the significant participation by community-based organizations in the collaboration, it is noteworthy that the deep-seated, historically embedded cynicism that so many community leaders felt toward the Chicago Initiative hardly deterred them from taking part.

Quite to the contrary, whether they saw the prize as a greater share of the summer funding pie or as getting funders to put substantial money behind their espoused commitments to revitalizing low-income neighborhoods, in both cases community leaders were able to keep their cynicism tucked far away in the hidden transcript. This enabled them, within the public transcript, to behave deferentially yet strategically toward funders. Community leaders outwardly affirmed the view that Chicago was especially prone to violence following the LA riots and thus needed a greater focus on programs for poor youth, while at the same time they tactically tried to work the terms of the collaboration more to their long-term advantage.

Chapter Five

Collaboration Becomes Old News

Long after the hoopla surrounding their distribution of summer grants in 1992 died down, there remained enthusiasm among many funders about trying to maintain the Chicago Initiative as a vehicle for antipoverty reform in the city. Their enthusiasm was fueled by the fact that the Long-Range Planning Task Force had spent the summer and fall of 1992 and the early months of 1993 trying, as we saw in Chapter Four, to piggyback upon sponsors' optimistic rhetoric from the very outset of the Chicago Initiative that the collaboration would thrive well beyond the crisis that propelled it to take action. Funders' enthusiasm also stemmed from the very different character that a second summer grants campaign took on in 1993.

THE 1993 SUMMER GRANTS CAMPAIGN

In April 1993, the Chicago Fund sent out invitations to community-based organizations to elicit their participation in a second summer campaign to expand programs for poor youth. In its efforts to raise funds from other foundations, the Chicago Fund drew on the same riot fears rhetoric that had been such a successful fundraising pitch the previous year. The Chicago Fund pointed out that a riot had in fact occurred the preceding summer on the night that the Chicago Bulls won the National Basketball Association championship for the second consecutive time (Chicago Initiative 1993a).[1]

Galvanizing support from other funders was difficult. The sense of panic that had inspired so many funders to come on board after the LA riots had long since dissipated since the media spotlight no longer focused on the riots and what they might mean for the 1992 presidential election. Moreover, the idea of distributing emergency summer grants was no longer new, and consequently did not carry a sense of urgency anymore for many funders. As a result, although there were actually more sponsors this time.

Table 6: Foundation Contributions to the 1993 Summer Grants Campaign

Type	Number	Dollars contributed (% of total)
Corporate	34	405,000 (29%)
Independent	7	995,000 (71%)
Total	41	1,400,000 (100%)

around, the Chicago Initiative raised only $1.4 million in 1993 compared to the $2.7 million raised in 1992 (See Table 6). [2]

Although funders as a whole perceived the threat of riots occurring in Chicago to have long since passed, the Chicago Fund still worked to convince other local foundations that they could gain significant visibility by supporting a second summer grantmaking campaign. This time around, the prestige would derive not from staving off riots but from collaborating with and allocating grants to community-based organizations that were not already "tapped into traditional information and funding networks," and which were working to revitalize low-income neighborhoods (Chicago Initiative 1993j:5). In a fundraising letter, the executive director of the Chicago Fund wrote, in reference to the 1992 summer grants campaign:

> [T]he participants in the Chicago Initiative did not concern themselves solely with the rapid response to the essential need for summer activities for youth. To their credit, the participants also determined to try to use their unique collaboration to develop a long-range plan for addressing the community, economic, and family development issues which are prevalent in the communities which the summer program was intended to serve. All involved in the Initiative have now determined that the continuation of this effort, including a second summer program, is essential (Chicago Initiative 1993k).

This fundraising pitch not only stemmed from the lukewarm response given by other foundations to the Chicago Fund's initial attempts to draw again on riot fears rhetoric; it also reflected criticisms voiced by grantees of how the summer 1992 grants had been allocated. This criticism stemmed from the fact that sponsors of the Chicago Initiative had given off the impression that funds would not go exclusively to the usual array of grantees—large, well established social-service agencies—and that even community-based organizations without prior ties to foundations would receive funding. Yet, this proved not to be the case as six downtown agencies collectively received 33.6 percent of the $2.4 million allocated and each of these agencies received grants from more than one of the four summer programming task forces. In contrast, neighborhood agencies received comparatively smaller grants from just one task force and not a single grassroots organization received summer 1992 funding from any task force.

In an interview, the director of a neighborhood agency explained how the summer 1992 grants criteria created unequal funding opportunities.

> We were asked to respond to a crisis with immediate programs, and a budget, and at the same time asked to make a prediction as to how it would work in the long term. It's just not possible. So many of us are already stretched way beyond our resources, putting in very long days. And then we're asked to keep administrative costs to a minimum. Who's going to supervise the programs, make sure they're being carried out effectively (Chicago Initiative 1993a:31)?

In a separate interview, the director of a downtown agency described the ease with which his organization was able to respond to the Chicago Initiative's call for grant proposals.

> We were able to respond very quickly when the [request for proposals] came around because these were all things we had, as a staff, begun to articulate as needs. So, when it came to putting together proposals, we were all ready to put proposals together because our machine was ready to do it anyway.

As the Chicago Initiative began allocating summer 1992 grants and as evidence of this inequality became glaringly obvious, the director of a religiously-affiliated grassroots organization, in a letter sent to the Chicago Fund staff person overseeing the grantmaking, expressed:

> There is some concern that a whole tier of grassroots organizing will again be left out of the networking of even the Chicago Initiative. Many of these church-based groups are too new and too community-

based to have been contacted, yet it would be an excellent thing if a certain amount of money could trickle all the way down to their level. Issues beyond jobs which are of primary concern to the churches seem to be: family, race and class relations, and community economic development. These are exactly the issues before the Long-Range Planning Task Force. How can we link religious-based community development efforts with the objectives of The Chicago Initiative (Chicago Initiative 1992p)?

Given that this kind of sentiment existed and given that pitching a second summer grants campaign to funders as a way to prevent riots would have been a hopeless cause, the Chicago Fund framed the 1993 grants campaign as a way for funders to show greater accountability to the less traditional, less established community-based organizations doing antipoverty work across the city. Consequently, the invitation sent to community-based organizations soliciting their involvement stated that this time around "[s]pecial attention [would] be paid to the long-range community development effort and the possibilities for collaborative efforts among agencies that this strategy affords" (Chicago Initiative 1993l).

And indeed, in contrast to the grant-giving pattern that emerged the previous summer, the 1993 summer campaign certainly lived up to its billing, as illustrated by Table 7. We can see that this time around, the piece of the pie allocated to downtown agencies dropped from 33.6% of the total in 1992 to 22.2% of the total in 1993. Furthermore, only four downtown agencies received grants from more than one of the programming task forces (Sports and Recreation, Arts and Culture, Jobs/Job Training, and Gang Intervention) in 1993. Caring for the Future, which received grants in 1992 from three task forces, did not receive a single 1993 grant.

Filling the gap were twenty-two neighborhood agencies, and twenty-three grassroots organizations. While neighborhood agencies each received one grant from the Chicago Initiative in 1992, some received multiple grants in 1993. All of the grassroots organizations funded were first-time grantees of the Initiative (Chicago Initiative 1993m). The 1993 grants, therefore, gave credibility to funders' broader claims of interest in revitalizing low-income neighborhoods: that they were committed to the idea of collaboration and to supporting unconventional antipoverty work.

Table 7: Comparison of Grants Distribution among Downtown Agencies between the Summer of 1992 and Summer of 1993

Grantee	1992 Amount	% of 1992 Total	Categories of 1992 Grants	1993 Amount	% of 1993 Total	Categories of 1993 Grants
Active Youth	$248,971	10.5	4	$58,189	4.2	2
Associated Agency	$159,325	6.7	4	$87,970	6.4	2
Concerned about Kids	$155,600	6.6	2	$64,000	4.7	3
Community United	$90,000	3.8	2	$63,463	4.7	2
Services for the Poor	$74,280	3.1	2	$30,000	2.2	1
Caring for the Future	$70,386	2.9	3	$0	0.0	0
TOTALS:	**$798,562**	**33.6**	2.8 (Mean)	303,622	22.2	1.3 (Mean)

FUNDING THE NEIGHBORHOOD REVITALIZATION AGENDA

And these were not merely *claims* of interest. For indeed, at the same time that the Chicago Initiative was disbursing 1993 summer grants, it was moving systematically toward acting upon recommendations made by the Long-Range Planning Task Force to allocate funds for the revitalization of poor neighborhoods in Chicago. In late June 1993, the task force held five "community conversations" with poor residents across the city. The purpose of these gatherings was both to collect information that would help in the implementation of a neighborhood revitalization agenda and to inform prospective grantees about this new source of funding.

The implementation of this agenda began in August 1993 when the Chicago Initiative sent a request for proposals to over 800 individuals and organizations across the city. The request sought for community-based organizations working in neighborhoods with poverty rates exceeding the citywide mean of 21.6 percent to collaborate on projects linking economic, community, and family development. There were three types of grants available, each of which was renewable for up to three years: a maximum of $35,000 for pre-development work, $50,000 in working capital for linking the three types of development, and unspecified amounts of non-monetary technical assistance.

Table 8: Neighborhood Revitalization Grants Awarded in March 2004

Grantee	Grant Category	Amount
Rebuilding the South Side	Pre-Development	$42,000
North Side Collaboration	Pre-Development	$10,000
Coalition for Families	Pre-Development	$35,000
Neighborhood Planners	Pre-Development	$35,000
United Community Rebuilders	Pre-Development	$35,000
Community Collaboration	Pre-Development	$35,000
Families and Communities United	Working Capital	$50,000

To apply for funding, prospective grantees had to send a letter of intent by September 24, 1993. Sixty-four organizations from 25 of the 27 communities eligible to apply sent such letters, of which 25 were given site visits and 12 were subsequently asked to submit full proposals by December 22, 1993. On January 24, 1994 the Distribution Committee approved the Long-Range Planning Task Force's 7 recommendations for funding, and the grants, totaling $242,000, were distributed in March 2004. Table 8 displays how these grants compared to one another in terms of their purpose and dollar amounts (Chicago Initiative 1993p, q, r, s, 1994l).

SHUTTING THE DOOR GRADUALLY

Rather than become the engine for eliciting subsequent neighborhood revitalization funding, these grants proved to be a momentary deviation from an incremental divestment of commitment to the Chicago Initiative. The summer of 1994 was fast approaching, and with it came the obvious question of whether the Initiative would launch a third summer grants campaign. Given the Chicago Initiative's 46 percent drop in fundraising between its 1992 and 1993 summer campaigns, the prospect of mustering sponsorship yet again seemed unlikely to the executive director of the Chicago Fund. After all, there was no longer a compelling impetus for funders to supplement, via the Chicago Initiative, their own separate summer programs for poor youth.

After the 1993 summer grants campaign, the Chicago Fund began to take on a posture of restrained support for the Chicago Initiative. Rather than formally abdicate the leadership role it had assumed since its very conception of the Initiative in the aftermath of the LA riots, the foundation simply proclaimed that it "was getting overcommitted on the Chicago Initiative projects" (Chicago Initiative 1993n). Consequently, the executive director of the Chicago Fund began to shift his energies to a different endeavor being undertaken by his organization—its recently conceived Children, Youth, and Families Initiative.

In October 1993, the Chicago Fund agreed to underwrite the costs of a strategic planning process for the Chicago Initiative. The Chicago Fund's executive director told me retrospectively in an interview, "I did not oppose doing strategic planning. You know, this thing kept snowballing along. It's pretty hard to say, 'No, we're not going to do it.'" At a Steering Committee meeting on November 8, 1993 he mentioned "the possibility of an endowment" for the Chicago Initiative (Chicago Initiative 1993o), however he did not indicate which funders would create it or how large it might be.

In September 1994, the Chicago Fund announced that it would scale back its leadership duties but still remain a "collaborative partner" (Chicago Initiative 1994l). Although the foundation made no mention of what its particular role within the collaboration would continue to be, the point to underscore here is that its actions continually gave the Long-Range Planning Task Force reason to keep devising ways of eliciting funders' support for its neighborhood revitalization agenda.

In January 1995, the Chicago Fund specified that it would designate a representative to the Initiative's Steering Committee and remain the fiscal agent responsible for receiving and administering grants (Chicago Initiative 1995e). This was yet another strategic move in which the foundation emphasized its continued *involvement* rather than how it was scaling back its commitments. Then, in March 1995, the Chicago Fund terminated its role as fiscal agent of the Chicago Initiative effective June 30, 1995, and announced that the Initiative would officially close on August 31 (Chicago Initiative 1995f). Just before it closed, the Initiative gave money to enable three of the seven collaborations that had been awarded neighborhood revitalization grants in January 1994 to receive two-year renewals at $30,000 a piece (Chicago Initiative 1995a).

All of the money for these neighborhood revitalization grants came from just one foundation, Madison Trust, which was a black sheep among the Chicago Initiative's sponsors in that it did not give any money to either of the two summer grants campaigns and was only interested in supporting long-range antipoverty reforms. The influence that Madison Trust exercised within Chicago philanthropy during the 1990s was so pronounced that a community leader who was actively involved on the Long-Range Planning Task Force commented, "I think the development of [the Chicago Initiative's] long-term plans never would have left the table had it not been for Madison Trust's persistence."

EXITING LOOKING GOOD

The fact that the Chicago Initiative *did* indeed follow through on its promise of funding a neighborhood revitalization agenda, coupled with the fact
that funders only gradually scaled back their commitments to the collaboration, explains how funders were able to cultivate, through the Initiative,
an image of social concern and responsibility. Consider the following comment made by a woman who served as a consultant to the Initiative:

> Were funders going to stand in the way of [this work] when it was
> driven by a bunch of people whom they had originally been working
> with? It sounds stupid to say, "No, we don't want to have any long-
> term plan. We just want to, you know, wing it here." So, they could
> very easily say, "Develop a plan and we'll consider it."

In a separate interview, the associate director of the Chicago Initiative similarly observed:

> I think if [the executive director of the Chicago Fund] had backed out
> earlier, he'd have been real criticized for putting fire insurance on the
> streets and that's it. People look to the Chicago Fund to provide con-
> vening leadership to support change. Staying on board shows that, in
> fact, he put in more money than others, and that other funding partners
> weren't there. This is a way for the Chicago Fund to legitimize its not
> hanging on forever, its getting out—the notion that they were commit-
> ted but others weren't. They supported this thing for two and a half
> years while at the same time sabotaging the process.

These comments reveal that even though they abandoned the collaboration, the Chicago Fund and the other foundations that supported it were
still able to come off looking good for having originally created the Initiative and sustained it for over three years. These funders were able to maintain a prestigious image even despite the fact that they did not support the
neighborhood revitalization agenda in the ways that the Long-Range Planning Task Force had envisioned. Indeed, these funders hardly gave off the
impression to the community leaders who took part in the collaboration
that the Initiative was merely a veiled, class-interested fire insurance policy
for downtown Chicago, as existing scholarship would suggest (Fisher
1983; Roelofs 2003).
  Moreover, it is crucial to emphasize that funders exercised the option
of not sustaining the collaboration only after they had shown considerable

excitement early on about the collaboration's long-range potential. One funder commented:

> There was never a commitment that the Chicago Initiative was going to go on forever, but there was also a feeling that if this was a one-time thing, and we're just going to do something, what are we accomplishing? All we're doing is a quick fix. There is no long-term benefit. So, there was the hope that it could develop into something—if not as a formal initiative, then at least continue to bring more money into Chicago neighborhoods from various foundations so that some of these things could continue to take place; either under the banner of the Initiative or without the banner of the Initiative. But, the long-term goal was certainly "there ought to be more money coming into Chicago communities."

Funders' decision not to sustain the collaboration was tacit rather than assertive. There were few times when a funder openly declared that it would not consider future support for the Chicago Initiative. Funders instead expressed their growing disinterest by placing less priority on planning meetings organized to discuss the neighborhood revitalization agenda. This meant that foundation executive directors stopped attending these meetings, yet at the same time they were still being represented at these meetings by lower-level program officers. These program officers gave the foundation visibility but held little authority to act on its behalf. In this regard, one community leader commented during an interview:

> I went to a meeting that was supposed to be the planning and oversight meeting and 90% of the people there—as a matter of fact, I made a sarcastic comment—90% of the people said "I'm Sally Smith representing commissioner so and so. I'm so and so representing so and so." And it was my turn and I said "I'm representing me and I want to know how come I am the only person here in a senior advisory position who comes to these meetings?"

For funders, maintaining a presence at meetings was part and parcel of their organizational identities. Sending staff to lengthy meetings was not only something that funders could afford to do, but reflected one of the things that funders do best. Madison Trust is a case in point. Prior to collecting the data for this study, I served for several months as a consultant to the foundation. My work revealed a lot about Madison Trust's approach to grantmaking since my job was to assemble information that a particular branch of the foundation was subsequently going to use to improve its grantmaking. The foundation saw my work as crucial since it required that I engage staff in an ongoing dialogue about what it wanted to accomplish and how.

Community-based organizations as a whole simply cannot afford to participate in this kind of dialogue. In relentless pursuit of funds to underwrite their programming and overhead costs, these organizations hesitated to become too committed to attending drawn-out meetings of the Chicago Initiative. A member of the Long-Range Planning Task Force who remained dedicated to the collaboration until the very end commented that "at first, getting closer to the funders was real exciting for a lot of people— you know, being able to just talk." However, community leaders' excitement started to diminish as they came to expect that talk would be followed by commitments of funding. When it became clear that these commitments would not be forthcoming, community leaders started to drop out of the planning process and the collaboration began to unravel.

WHY FUNDERS DID NOT STAY COMMITTED

Sponsors' reluctance to stay committed to the Chicago Initiative can be explained by returning to the context in which this collaboration came into being in the first place. Following the LA riots, a group of funders joined together to define the need for action. Although funders pitched their actions as a response to community-based fears of riots, their efforts were *not* in truth community-initiated. As we saw in Chapter Four, the community leaders who attended early meetings of the Chicago Initiative expressed fears of riots as a strategic way of justifying the need for emergency grants at a time when their organizations were particularly desperate for funds. In this regard, the Chicago Initiative had local historical precedent, as a veteran community activist explained in an interview. "I don't know of any initiative in Chicago ever where funders decided to respond to a need expressed in a community and created something like an initiative or collaboration." Indeed, among the scores of comprehensive community initiatives created nationwide during the 1980s and 1990s, every single one of them was sponsor-driven (Brown and Garg 1997).

The fact that sponsors were the ones who conceived these initiatives and subsequently presented community-based organizations with invitations to take part meant that funders implicitly defined the terms upon which they would collaborate. In the case of the Chicago Initiative, funders had twin motives for participating. On the one hand, they were morally interested in collaborating with community-based organizations since, at the time of the Chicago Initiative, collaboration was widely viewed throughout the philanthropic world as the best vehicle for ameliorating poverty. This motive derived from foundations' longstanding institutional aim to mitigate social problems, an aim that garnered newfound credibility through the policymaking roles foundations assumed in the wake of the federal government downsizing that began in the 1980s. On the other hand, sponsors were instrumentally interested in gaining prestige among community-based organizations by looking good for coming to the aid of the poor amidst a crisis.

So long as these two motives remained mutually compatible, funders remained committed to the Chicago Initiative. But as time went by, acting morally became increasingly detached from the media spotlight that enabled funders to look good in the aftermath of the LA riots. Consequently, funders' actions demonstrated that their instrumental motive trumped their moral motive. Their commitments to the Chicago Initiative increasingly became centered on talking about the neighborhood revitalization agenda rather than allocating funds to support this agenda.

Funders defined their commitments to the Chicago Initiative by drawing on two criteria that foundations conventionally use for deciding whether or not to award a grant. The first, *getting bang for the buck*, pertains to whether there is evidence that the grant will sufficiently meet specified, quantitatively measurable goals. The second, *being on the cutting edge of grantmaking*, involves supporting programs that are new, innovative, and different from what has been funded before.

Getting Bang for the Buck

The community leader who served as executive director of the New Futures Initiative—a comprehensive community initiative undertaken in Savannah, Little Rock, Dayton, Pittsburgh, and Lawrence, Massachusetts—described how the sponsor of this initiative, the Annie E. Casey Foundation, placed strong emphasis on getting bang for the buck:

> On the one hand, Casey sent the message, "This is about systems change." But then on the other hand, they gave us a guidebook for our proposals that seemed to be saying, "You must have case management," which is clearly direct service. "You should have a youth employability system," which usually meant new services. "And you've got to reach these benchmarks: You must decrease dropouts by X percent, and teen pregnancies by Y percent, and something else by this percent over these five years" (Quoted in Walsh 1999:4)

Consider how the desire to get bang for the buck similarly played out in foundations' responses to requests for funding support of the Chicago Initiative's neighborhood revitalization agenda. In a letter, the executive director of the Warble Foundation answered such a request by stating:

> You asked if Warble could consider a restricted grant to the long-range component. To do so, we would need to know more about what is actually planned, hoped-for results, time frame, and what costs need to be covered. Your March 1993 report "Communities That Work" contains a long list of long range recommendations but I don't think these are suggested as a work plan for the next 12 months—more a wish list (Chicago Initiative 1993t).

Across the board, as we saw in Chapter Three, sponsors emphatically claimed an interest in supporting a new kind of antipoverty reform in which partnerships with poor constituencies would contribute toward building these constituencies' capacity to revitalize their own distressed neighborhoods. However, sponsors came to see that community building would take considerably longer than they had expected, with their "expectations" implicitly defined around traditional funding practices in which grants last no more than one to three years in duration. Sponsors of comprehensive community initiatives tacitly recognized that prolonged funding commitments were needed for their collaborations to make meaningful long-term impacts. However, it is virtually unheard of for foundations to make such commitments. The fact that within a few comprehensive community initiatives (not Chicago) sponsors were willing to commit funds for five years was therefore itself an unprecedented philanthropic practice (Brown and Garg 1997; Kubisch 1996).

Making short-term, rather than prolonged and open-ended, funding commitments is one way for foundations to ensure that grants achieve what they set out to do. If after a grant expires there are few indicators of success, the funder will likely opt not to renew the grant. This practice helps foundations attain more bang for the buck than if they initially make longer-term funding commitments. In conjunction with their proclivity for awarding shorter-term grants, foundations also typically require that a grant proposal include quantitative assessments of the kinds of results that the grant can be expected to yield. This might include estimates of the number of jobs that the grant will create or of the percentage that the grant will decrease neighborhood crime.

Given that comprehensive community initiatives set in motion long-term antipoverty agendas that were not easily measurable, in the case of

Chicago, from very early on many funders saw their ongoing support of the collaboration as contingent upon community leaders producing evidence that funders would get bang for their buck. As we saw in Chapter Four, the community activists who comprised the Long-Range Planning Task Force worked with this goal explicitly in mind. The task force went to great lengths to package its agenda as an extension of the short-term, discretely measurable antipoverty work that foundations typically sponsor, which was precisely the kind of work that galvanized the creation of the Chicago Initiative.

Despite its efforts, the Long-Range Planning Task Force's strategic work ultimately proved unconvincing as sponsors did not see the neighborhood revitalization agenda as providing enough bang for the level of investment being asked of them. At the Chicago Initiative's final meeting in July 1995, the chief reason cited for ending the collaboration was the "inability to communicate a clear vision of TCI with specific outcomes that would elicit strong support from policy makers and other potential partners" (Chicago Initiative 1995a)

A recurring sentiment expressed by funders was that the neighborhood revitalization agenda simply did not cohere with the short-term, riot-prevention goals that had originally driven the collaboration to come together—goals that, not coincidentally, yielded lots of bang for the buck. In a letter to the Chicago Initiative's executive director in February 1994, the executive director of United Philanthropies wrote:

> I find the issue of the mission of the Initiative to be particularly murky. As an individual who, until fairly recently, was involved as a participant only in the initial formative meetings, I thought the Initiative was focused on opportunities for youth. Then I more recently heard that the focus has shifted more toward a long-range goal of ameliorating embedded community poverty with summer, year-round, and long range components. I think this shift—while it may be appealing and worthy of pursuit—is a primary source of the current difficulty. The long term mission is an enormously ambitious and imposing purpose, and one which does not easily or comfortably tie back into the initial summer youth crisis focus that still is the central glue holding a significant part of the Initiative's constituency together (Chicago Initiative 1994m).

In an interview, the chair of the Chicago Initiative's Distribution Committee similarly conveyed why there was reluctance among foundations to commit funds to the neighborhood revitalization agenda.

> This is tough stuff—this community-building stuff. I mean, it's hard to describe, it's hard to get your arms around. If you're a funder, it's hard

to understand how your $20,000—what it's exactly going to do. And funders want to know that stuff. It's hard to convince your board that you need to do this for the next ten years. The culture, the institutional history of foundations just sort of argues against that.

The executive director of Businesses for the Greater Good was quite explicit in claiming, moreover, that funding the neighborhood revitalization agenda would not enable foundations to cultivate organizational prestige in the way that supporting summer riot prevention programs most certainly did.

> I think there was a lot of pondering at the time, a lot of thinking at the time, "is this thing [the neighborhood revitalization agenda] for real or is it kind of a solution of the week type of thing? You know, everybody is going to rally up and we're going to [fund the revitalization of poor neighborhoods] and in 2–3 years it will be gone and there won't be anything to show for it. And why should we put money into this as opposed to some initiatives that we're developing in-house that we can get visibility for and that are going to be established as our programs versus a collaborative program?"

Although in hindsight it might be tempting to see sponsors' reluctance to sustain the Chicago Initiative as an indication that this initiative was simply a slick public relations endeavor, it is crucial that we view foundations' actions within the institutional context in which they unfolded. Sponsors' reluctance to make open-ended funding commitments had roots that can only properly be understood by getting inside foundation culture. This is a culture in which pragmatic concerns guide grantmaking much more than ideological concerns, and chief among these pragmatic concerns is whether there is tangible evidence upon which to justify giving away money.

These pragmatic concerns derive from the very organizational structures that characterized the foundations that participated in the Chicago Initiative. Whether these foundations were independent or corporate, their boards were comprised largely of people from the business world (Odendahl 1987) and the organizations embraced business models of operation. Indeed, the parallels between grantmaking culture and business culture are striking. In an ethnographic study of several corporations, Jackall (1988) documented that managers have strong career-based incentives to seek out short-term rather than long-term solutions to the problems they encounter. The exigencies of managers' daily work require that they direct their attention to immediate problems since doing so best ensures that they will be able to demonstrate to their superiors and their peers that they are making measurable progress and getting tangible positive results from their work.

Being on the Cutting Edge

In addition to their stance that neighborhood revitalization grants would not yield much bang for the buck, Chicago foundations were also hesitant to make long-term funding commitments that might constrain them from allocating other kinds of grants in the future. In other words, they were reluctant to tie up their money in a single project that would gradually cease being novel, when they could instead spread the money across a number of continually innovative projects.

Foundations routinely make efforts to be on the cutting edge of grant-making, and they view these efforts as integral to their distinct organizational identities. Most foundations prefer to be at the forefront of supporting new projects—a preference that drives their interest in providing seed money rather than allocating the funds necessary to sustain projects over time. Wanting to be on the cutting edge was explicitly what led the Spradler Foundation to support only the Chicago Initiative's two summer grants campaigns, as its executive director explained in a letter.

> Through our fiscal year 1993 and fiscal year 1994 grants, we have been pleased to provide the seed money which helped to make the development of the Chicago Initiative possible. However, we consider the $150,000 which these grants represent to be "start-up" funds to give the Initiative time to diversify its funding base by seeking support from other sources (Chicago Initiative 1993u).

The Chicago Initiative came into being in large part because its various sponsors viewed pooling money for emergency violence prevention grants as cutting-edge. The idea of joining forces to respond to a crisis was out of the ordinary. For this reason, the 27 foundations that supported the summer 1992 grants campaign and the 41 that funded the 1993 campaign allocated moneys without the lengthy bureaucratic process that grantmaking often involves. This was particularly the case in 1992 since the Chicago Initiative came together just weeks after the LA riots. Sponsors allocated funds to the Initiative by exercising an emergency prerogative allowing for programming staff to award grants without prior approval from the board of trustees.

While sponsors saw the emergency pooling together of funds as cutting-edge, they had no comparable motivation for extending their commitments to the Chicago Initiative. In sponsors' eyes, sustaining the Chicago Initiative would have required creating a new bureaucratic apparatus that subsequently would have become just another player in a crowded field of grant seekers vying for their money. This was something that foundations emphatically did not want to support, which is why sponsorship declined as the Initiative moved away from the sense of urgency that had surrounded the summer violence-prevention grants, and toward more mundane organizational matters such as securing office space and hiring staff. Reflecting back on the Chicago Initiative in an interview conducted less than a year after its closing, the Chicago Fund staff person who directed the Initiative's two summer campaigns commented:

> I think part of the excitement of the Chicago Initiative was that voluntary commitment that was created. It was ad-hoc. In the second year, it quite naturally moved toward the question, "how do you begin to try to build it to sustain it?" I think that's probably, in large measure, what [the Initiative's executive director] saw as her job. She tried to tighten up some of the committee structure, had a larger staff budget, etc. It may have been that the strength of the Chicago Initiative was more in its ad-hoc nature, and less in its institutional nature, such as it might have been, and institutionalizing it, then, potentially created a separate set of interests.

Foundations' desire to be on the cutting edge of grantmaking produced an ironic set of circumstances. Although in principle sponsors bought into the Chicago Initiative's neighborhood revitalization vision and recognized that summer violence-prevention grants would, by themselves, not fulfill that vision, they saw funding these grants as more palatable than creating a new entity to pursue that vision. In an interview, the executive director of the Care Foundation explained this irony:

> I think it wasn't so much that people in foundations were indifferent to the community needs, because I don't think that's true. I think people still really cared about the kind of community services they were giving, but I think it has to do with what happened to the Initiative. It became a structure itself. We were paying salaries, we were paying rent, there were job descriptions, there were utility costs—all of those things that go into operating an entity. There was an organizational, an overhead component, and then it gets right back into the old processes, the old routines for giving away money. And I think that's one thing that bogged it down.

As the Chicago Initiative gradually instituted the level of bureaucracy that was necessary to build a sustainable collaboration, sponsors began to see the Initiative as just another organization vying for their money. Since the Initiative was an intermediary between funders and grantees, sponsors believed that the money required to finance its administrative costs could be more productively utilized if given directly to grantees that already had formal organizational structures in place. In a letter to the executive director of the Chicago Fund, the executive director of the Comak Foundation cited this as its reason for only contributing $50,000 to the Initiative in 1993, compared to the $100,000 it gave the year before. Moreover, the Comak Foundation's executive director expressed ambivalence about making future contributions to the Initiative:

> Our 1993 contribution to the United Way of Chicago will be $1 million, while the [Chicago] area will receive close to $4.5 million from Amoco. While we cannot honor your request for $100,000, we are pleased to enclose a check for $50,000 to assist you in bringing people together to address deep-rooted problems and achieve tangible results. Long-term we are concerned about the duplication in supporting the Initiative, given our present level of support to United Way and direct support to many of the participating organizations.

Even Madison Trust, the sole contributor of funds to the Chicago Initiative's neighborhood revitalization agenda, refrained from becoming too committed to the Initiative because the foundation had its own long-range antipoverty programs in place. It was one thing for the foundation to fund the Initiative's neighborhood revitalization work and then to renew these grants once the decision had been officially made to disband the collaboration. However, it was a wholly different matter for the foundation to fund an entirely new collaboration when the foundation could be more on the cutting edge of antipoverty grantmaking by allocating grants on its own. Hence, by the beginning of 1995 Madison Trust's behavior came to resemble that of its peers, and foundation interest in the Chicago Initiative continued to wane. The writing was on the wall and the collaboration disbanded the following summer.

EVALUATING THE SUCCESSES OF THE CHICAGO INITIATIVE

During the more than three years that the Chicago Initiative lasted, it allocated approximately $3.5 million during the two summer violence prevention campaigns and another $332,000 to support the neighborhood revitalization agenda. In addition to these dollar amounts, the Chicago Initiative was also instrumental in fostering a whole array of new social relationships across Chicago's philanthropic community. These relationships had two positive effects for community-based organizations. First, these organizations moved into better position to leverage foundation funding, and second, these organizations built layers of solidarity with one another to a degree that had not existed previously.

Leveraging Foundation Funding

It will make sense why the Chicago Initiative enabled community-based organizations to gain greater access to foundation funding if we first underscore the fact that funders were as morally committed to the imperative to revitalize low-income neighborhoods as were community activists. It was just that funders drew upon traditional grantmaking criteria in deciding how they would act upon their morals. In an interview, one sponsor reflected upon how the disjuncture between foundations' principled interests in antipoverty reform and their organizational cultures played out in their fleeting commitments to the Chicago Initiative:

> There was never a commitment that The Chicago Initiative was going to go on forever, but there was also a feeling that if this was a one-time thing, and we're just going to do something, what are we accomplishing? All we're doing is a quick fix. There is no long-term benefit. So, there was the hope that it could develop into something—if not as a formal initiative, then at least continue to bring more money into Chicago neighborhoods from various foundations so that some of these things could continue to take place; either under the banner of the Initiative or without the banner of the Initiative. But, the long-term goal was certainly "there ought to be more money coming into Chicago communities."

Hence, for foundations the drawback of sustaining the Chicago Initiative did not lie in funding the neighborhood revitalization agenda but in *collaboratively* funding this agenda.

It is telling that after the Chicago Initiative discontinued and foundations returned to their normative practice of allocating their own separate grants, foundations remained interested in funding neighborhood revitalization efforts. This interest enabled those grantees that had been the recipients of neighborhood revitalization grants from the Initiative to leverage other moneys even after the collaboration had disbanded. A member of the Long-Range Planning Task Force observed:

> We saw a couple of the collaborations we funded get a higher profile and leverage other funds from other foundations because they had gotten Chicago Initiative funds. They became better known in different circles because of our support.

As an illustration, consider that while North Side Collaboration received a pre-development grant from the Chicago Initiative of just $10,000, the value of that grant proved considerably larger. Since the sponsors of the Initiative were some of the largest foundations in the city, being able to list a Chicago Initiative grant on subsequent grant proposals added immensely to a grantee's future fundraising prospects. And sure enough, several months after receiving money from the Chicago Initiative, North Side Collaboration became one of just 20 organizations to receive a $500,000 grant from the U.S. Department of Labor to develop innovative school-to-work antipoverty programs (Chicago Initiative 1995g).

In an interview about a year after the Initiative disbanded, a staff member of the Chicago Fund commented that the Long-Range Planning Task Force's vision for antipoverty reform throughout the city was still coming to some fruition, just in a piecemeal fashion rather than via an ongoing collaborative structure:

> **Staff member:** One of the good things that has come out of [the Chicago Initiative] is that I still deal with organizations which were given those early moneys in the first two summers whose programs were changed by those activities. And now, I get requests from organizations, in my annual round of funding which still have a strong Chicago Initiative component to them. It also put us in touch with a lot of very small, basic grassroots organizations that we normally wouldn't deal with. So, it gave me a sense of a whole level of activity that I had not been aware of. You know, we're a big, old, very well established foundation that funds the larger, more stable organizations, and for the most part wasn't dealing a lot with these little community efforts.
>
> **IS:** So, you're saying that some of those new contacts have been sustained?
>
> **Staff member:** Absolutely.
>
> **IS:** Some of these organizations have been funded?
>
> **Staff member:** Absolutely. And we continue to fund them. And they continue to provide jobs and different kinds of activities for young people in communities of need. That for me is the long-range plan of the Chicago Initiative.

Participating in the Chicago Initiative enabled community-based organizations that were previously unknown to foundations to become better networked, and consequently to move into position to tap new sources of grant money, as another Chicago Fund staff person commented.

> I think that the thing that was most positive for the Chicago Fund was its introduction to a whole lot of people, and a lot of potential grantees that, I suspect, in the normal course of events they wouldn't have known. There is, as you well know, a barrier between the foundations and the real small, marginal, neighborhood-based organization. The latter doesn't feel it can get a fair and good hearing from the former.

As part of the Chicago Fund's Children, Youth, and Families Initiative, the foundation funded two organizations that had received 1993 summer funding from the Chicago Initiative. The staff person just quoted characterized these first-time grantees as organizations that "wouldn't have gotten a very receptive hearing at the Chicago Fund in the normal, pre-Initiative days because their styles were a little raggedy and confrontational."

It is of course difficult, based on this study alone, to ascertain how extensively the Chicago Initiative collaboration expanded the social networks of community-based organizations that had previously experienced difficulty accessing foundation funding. What can be established, however, is that there remained strong funder interest in long-range antipoverty reform well after the Chicago Initiative disbanded. This interest continued in larg part because the collaboration itself no longer remained as a structural impediment to funders acting in ways that yielded their *own* bang for the buck.

Building Strength through Numbers

Besides enabling community-based organizations to leverage wider foundation funding, the Chicago Initiative also offered these organizations the opportunity to build relationships with other nonprofits doing antipoverty work that they rarely interacted with previously. In an interview, the head of a downtown agency indicated that "there are several major partnerships around this town that took place as a result of the Initiative and all had their beginnings through the Chicago Initiative." In a separate interview, the executive director of a community development corporation similarly commented:

> Since the Chicago Initiative, I have gotten much more involved with social service agencies in the same neighborhood that I do community development activity. I don't think I would have done that had it not been for the work I had done for the Chicago Initiative.

The person who coordinated the Initiative's 1992 summer grants campaign pointed out in an interview that the creation of these new networks among community-based organizations was an unanticipated positive consequence of the collaboration.

> We have Associated Agency sitting across the table from James Thornton of Strive to Survive, which is a small informal community group in Englewood talking about gangs and gang work. I mean here's the head of a major nonprofit talking to a very small grassroots leader. And they developed those kinds of relationships. So, for me that was a benefit that nobody had expected to derive—that these other relationships beyond the funding relationship would occur. And I think that was—for me—one of the important things beyond how much money was out there.

If we were to measure the success of the Chicago Initiative strictly in terms of how much money it raised or how successfully community-based organizations leveraged foundation grants once the collaboration disbanded, we would miss the less tangible, but no less significant, benefits that these organizations accrued by participating. A member of the Long-Range Planning Task Force summed up these benefits by commenting:

> Although we tend to evaluate such efforts like TCI based on concrete outcomes, the real value of this type of collaboration is what happens between the collaborative partners and the relationships that develop. People participate in TCI because they are passionate about this city and believe collectively we can forge a new direction for impacting persistent poverty in Chicago (Chicago Initiative 1994b).

This comment points to the fact that the new relationships community-based organizations fostered with one another were, in their own right, an important marker of the success of the Chicago Initiative. These relationships positioned community-based organizations so that they could maximize their utilization of the various resources *other than money*—such as labor, skill, commitment, and trust—that are needed to improve the conditions of the poor (McCarthy and Zald 1977; Oberschall 1973; Tilly 1978). These relationships also served to validate a deep-seated conviction held by community activists that the indigenous strength of their organizations could, in and of itself, go a long way toward helping to mitigate the devastating effects of urban poverty (Gold 1997; Green 1997; Morris 1984).

Section III
Giving a Little, Getting a Lot

Chapter Six

Unmasking Collaboration

In critically evaluating the Chicago Initiative, it is tempting to see it simply as just another among a series of similar historical examples where policy elites created hoopla and fanfare around promises of funding to ameliorate poverty, and then abandoned those promises. Viewed in this way, the Chicago Initiative shares something fundamental in common with the federal war on poverty of the 1960s.

One oft-made criticism of that earlier effort was that, although it created community action agencies in order to elicit the maximum feasible participation of poor constituencies in antipoverty reforms, in time these agencies got co-opted by municipal elites. For example, Chicago Mayor Richard J. Daley, in believing that the city's community action agency would recklessly allow the poor to use federal funds to defy the local political machine, consequently proclaimed himself as the agency's leader. He proceeded to appoint several middle-class blacks to serve as representatives of the poor on its board, and through his efforts ensured that the money the federal government channeled to Chicago to reform local institutions and empower the poor would accomplish neither of these goals (Adler 1994; Patterson 2000; Zarefsky 1986).

Drawing this kind of comparison between the Chicago Initiative and the war on poverty is consistent with how previous sociological studies have characterized the relationship between foundations and community-based organizations. The data from these studies, which pertain chiefly to foundation support for the civil rights movement, reveal that funders exhibited a growing preference to support politically moderate organizations, such as the NAACP, as the movement splintered and as other organizations like SNCC increasingly became militant, defiant, and openly confrontational in their organizing tactics. Foundations overwhelmingly preferred to support moderates as a way of simultaneously giving these groups legitimacy and financially suffocating the movement's radical factions. This pattern of foundation funding gave community-based organizations motivation to channel their tactics toward institutionally acceptable forms of protest. In this way, foundations co-opted the civil rights movement to promote forms of social change that were consistent with their own class-based interests (Haines 1984, 1988; Jenkins and Eckert 1986; McAdam 1982; Piven and Cloward 1977).

The Chicago Initiative fits this general sociological pattern in several respects. Its sponsors allocated millions of dollars for riot prevention grants yet gave little for programs aimed to effect more systemic changes in the lives of the city's poor population—programs that, if implemented on a large scale, might have indirectly undermined foundations' class interests. Moreover, although funders never said so explicitly in the interviews that I conducted with them, it is reasonable to infer that their actions were motivated to some, or perhaps to a large, extent by fears that riots would devastate the material interests of Chicago's elite. After all, the Initiative's sponsors were organizations whose boards, like those of most foundations across the U.S., were comprised largely of people recruited from the business world (Odendahl 1987).

There is historical precedent for making this inference that sponsorship of the Initiative was, at its core, a way for the philanthropic elite to put a fire insurance policy on the streets of Chicago. Consider that one-third of the businesses that created urban affairs departments across the country during the late 1960s, a time of unparalleled rioting, claimed to have done so explicitly as a form of "insurance" (Haines 1988). Similarly, a detailed account of the 1968 riots in Chicago reports that whites in downtown just a few miles east of the fires "could see the smoke" while other whites, " twenty miles from Lawndale [a site of rioting], barricaded their suburban homes and waited" (Farber 1988). It is no wonder, then, that one of the community leaders I interviewed characterized the sponsors of the Chicago Initiative as motivated primarily by an interest in "keeping their businesses going and in keeping the city from going up in smoke which would create an environment that was going to affect profits."

In a different interview another community leader, reflecting back on her activism in Chicago since being involved in the feminist movement during the 1960s, pointed out that the Chicago Initiative was consistent with another local trend:

> I don't know of any initiative in Chicago ever where funders decided to respond to a need expressed in a community and created something like an initiative or a collaboration. I don't know of one example where they succeeded. Now, if these same social-service agencies, out of concern

about violence and all the rest of it, had said that "you know what, we've got to have a citywide effort; we've got to go to the meetings and we've got to figure this out; we've got to go to the funders collectively because we've got to be able to say we need the money to be able to do this"—then I think it would have been a wholly different animal.

This historical reference paints the Chicago Initiative as an elite-driven effort to maintain law and order within poor neighborhoods explicitly for the funders' own sake, as opposed to its being an effort that responded to needs and concerns originally conceived and voiced wholly by poor constituencies.

CO-OPTATION THROUGH NEGOTIATION

The historical narrative of the Chicago Initiative presented in the preceding three chapters does considerably more than just corroborate existing sociological perspectives about foundation co-optation, which see foundations as having a tendency to channel the goals of community-based organizations that work to effect social justice for disenfranchised populations. This study highlights, moreover, how an insidious form of co-optation occurs within *collaborations,* which are the unique social contexts that characterized the more than fifty comprehensive community initiatives created during the 1980s and 1990s. Co-optation, within these contexts, is insidious because it occurs at the very same time that funders are negotiating the terms of their relationship with prospective grantees. Although the collaboration model originally came about with a purported sensitivity toward avoiding undue elite influence, strictly by design this model has not been able to circumvent the possibility of co-optation taking place (Jones 2003).

In the particular case of the Chicago Initiative, it was precisely because the collaboration enabled community-based organizations to assert significant influence over foundation funding priorities that foundations were able to legitimately channel the bulk of their funding toward summer violence prevention grants instead of targeting the long-range revitalization of poor neighborhoods. The historical details of the Chicago Initiative reveal that its conceptual importance would be lost if we saw it *simply* as another tale of foundation co-optation. After all, the Chicago Initiative did not just come together to prevent riots and then immediately disband. Rather, the collaboration lasted more than three years—well beyond the crisis that originally propelled it into action—before it finally came undone.

During this time, amidst their efforts to look socially responsible for trying to prevent the riot-induced fires that ignited in LA from spreading to Chicago, funders felt heat from the community leaders with whom they were collaborating. Particularly those community leaders who comprised the Long-Range Planning Task Force recognized that the sense of crisis that spawned the creation of the Initiative also fostered the opportunity for them to gain new concessions from funders. This finding supports other research on community partnerships, which shows that groups empowered by these partnerships are able to assert influence in ways that procure them concrete advantages (Jones 2003).

Funders' image-building campaign, therefore, created a situation analogous to what Kingdon (1995) calls a "policy window" and Jones (2003) calls a "political space"—a situation in which an interest group (in this case, community-based organizations) is presented with a fruitful opportunity to exert influence over policy decisions. In the case of the Chicago Initiative, these organizations became empowered to make funders' actions concerning the Initiative's neighborhood revitalization agenda accord with their identity claims. The fact that funders opened themselves up to manipulation at the very same time that they bolstered their prestige characterized the paradoxical manner that the Initiative enabled funders to negotiate their power as means toward co-opting the Chicago Initiative's agenda.

Gaining access to the divergent social worlds of foundations and community-based organizations allowed me to become privy to this paradox. This access enabled me to develop Ostrander and Schervish's (1990) call for empirical analysis of funder-grantee relationships and the multiple layers of power they contain. Over the course of the Chicago Initiative, these relationships were not structured simply according to who held the purse strings. Indeed, community-based organizations also had significant cards to play. They carried the power to hold sponsors accountable to long-range funding promises they had made at the outset of the collaboration amidst their efforts to piggyback on the media attention generated by the LA riots and look good for preventing a similar scenario from occurring in Chicago. By including community leaders within the Chicago Initiative's decision-making structure, funders fueled a process in which their new partners became legitimate spokespersons for the possible directions that the Initiative might take. Indeed, funders' efforts to gain prestige among community-based organizations carried political resources that community leaders sought to exploit to their own advantage.

COMPARING THE RHETORIC AND THE REALITY OF PHILANTHROPIC COLLABORATION

Inclusiveness was the distinctive hallmark of comprehensive community initiatives, given that the norm within philanthropy has traditionally been exclusivity: a foundation issues a request for proposals, prospective grantees apply for funding, and the foundation then decides more-or-less unilaterally how to disperse its moneys. But, what exactly do philanthropists' claims of fostering "inclusiveness" through collaboration mean? Of central sociological importance here is the disjuncture between the rhetoric and reality of collaboration.

In both Chicago and elsewhere, sponsors of comprehensive community initiatives projected images of funders and community leaders sitting side by side at the negotiating table participating equally in formulating antipoverty reforms. And in the case of the Chicago Initiative, there was certainly some evidence to uphold this image. Consider that at the official kickoff meeting of the Chicago Initiative in June 1992, there were more than three hundred people in attendance from all different types of organizations whose work affected low-income populations. This incredible turnout prompted one African American social-service agency director, in an interview, to describe the meeting as "the greatest gathering of grassroots community leaders in the city since Dr. [Martin Luther] King was shot. I saw every community activist I'd ever met in my life there." Furthermore, community leaders comprised the majority of the Chicago Initiative's summer programming task forces, which made funding recommendations in the areas of sports & recreation, arts & culture, gang intervention, and jobs/job training. In most cases, the Distribution Committee, comprised of funders, did not challenge but rather rubber-stamped these task forces' grant recommendations.

However, I came across a noteworthy exception to this rule that involved the Initiative's Gang Intervention Task Force. The members of this task force were divided over how effectively they believed different kinds of community-based organizations were in carrying out gang intervention work in low-income neighborhoods. One task force member told me that several others did not think that certain downtown agencies should be funded because they were unfamiliar with the array of dangers involved in doing gang intervention work. However, this sentiment could not comfortably be shared with other task force members that worked for these particular agencies. Moreover, since it had become known that the Distribution Committee generally preferred to fund downtown agencies, the task force had its hands tied. The person who recounted this story emphasized that if downtown agencies were not on the final list of grant recommendations given to the Distribution Committee, then the committee would not support these recommendations. Thus, the particular downtown agencies in question were put onto the grantee list and the committee subsequently approved it.

Therefore, although it appeared that the Gang Intervention Task Force held grantmaking power in that here was an instance in which its grant recommendations were "rubber stamped," the fact that the Distribution Committee retained final say in grant decisions limited the task force's range of grantmaking options. Even though the Distribution Committee usually approved the summer programming task forces' choices of grantees, this committee still retained a measure of grantmaking power, which the Chicago Initiative's collaborative structure euphemized. Euphemisms are words and behaviors that serve to mask the power that certain groups hold over others (Bourdieu 1977; Edelman 1974; Scott 1989). In the case at hand, the rhetoric and practice of collaboration veiled the extent to which foundations' power over community-based organizations remained largely unchanged by comprehensive community initiatives.[1]

Indeed, to a significant degree the reality of collaboration did not correspond with the rhetoric. In this regard Atkinson (1999: 60), in a critical analysis of collaborations that aimed to foster community empowerment in the UK, writes:

> . . . the mere existence of an official discourse advocating empowerment and partnership is no guarantee that it will actually be translated into practice in an unmediated fashion *or* that the intention of such a discourse is *genuinely* to empower communities through participation in urban regeneration partnerships. Thorough-going empowerment of communities is unlikely, not least because of the confusion which surrounds these terms, but equally because the organisational contexts in which discursive practices operate are also sites of power relationships and contestation.

In the case of the Chicago Initiative, although the collaboration transformed the status of community-based organizations, who are traditionally outsiders to the grantmaking process, collaboration did not enable them to become the core insiders to this process that funders' rhetoric had claimed they would become. More accurately, community-based organizations' change of status was merely cosmetic. They became peripheral insiders, holding a seat at the table and occupying a legitimate role as policymaker but exercising only symbolic power in relation to the core insiders—the funders—sitting alongside of them (Maloney, Jordan, and McLaughlin 1994).

We have already seen how this was true with respect to the Chicago Initiative's summer grants. Since there was agreement among partners on the need to fund the specific programming agenda (violence prevention), the collaboration largely focused on how to implement this agenda; in other words, which organizations to fund. The story recounted above concerning the Gang

Intervention Task Force reveals that funders retained a certain level of grantmaking power that they did not share equally with their purported partners, leaving community leaders to some degree on the periphery. Community leaders' insider status in formulating the neighborhood revitalization agenda was even more peripheral. Here, the collaboration never proceeded toward discussions about implementation because funders and community leaders were not in alignment about the need to fund this agenda in the first place.

While the Long-Range Planning Task Force strived arduously to get funders on board, the truth of the matter was that this task force held little genuine negotiating power. Ultimately, foundations decided on their own— *not* in partnership with community leaders—about the utility of pursuing this agenda. The fact that their purported partners had come up with compelling reasons to maintain the collaboration and fund this agenda seemed to matter little, and ultimately fell on deaf ears. This illustration of the different degrees of insider status that community-based organizations occupied within the Chicago Initiative's two programming agendas is consistent with the findings of other research about collaboration, which reveals that community influence tends to be more extensive in terms of policy implementation than in terms of policy design (Taylor 2001).[2]

OLD WINE IN NEW BOTTLES

The story of the Chicago Initiative does not simply illustrate the failure of philanthropic collaboration practices to live up to their espoused rhetoric about inclusiveness and equality of decision-making influence. Moreover, the collaboration itself reproduced the very power disparities between foundations and community-based organizations that it purported to mitigate. The Chicago Initiative reinforced existing inequalities between the two groups by setting them up to occupy incommensurately different levels of insider status, which amounted to a similar state of affairs as traditionally exists within philanthropy, wherein there is a fundamental distinction between those with insider status (grantmakers) and those with outsider status (grantees).

Looked at in this way, the Chicago Initiative collaboration merely poured old wine into new bottles, and by doing so, conveyed the underlying message to its participants that there are structurally defined limits to the degree of democracy that is possible within philanthropy. Since a similar disjuncture between rhetoric and reality existed across comprehensive community initiatives (*Voices from the Field* 1997), the collaboration model itself reinforced existing funder-grantee disparities by tacitly affirming that the only inroads toward democratic philanthropy that were reasonable were those that were being practiced. And by reproducing existing inequalities in this way, the collaboration legitimized the very existence of these inequalities by providing funders with justification for placing limits on what they thought was possible, thereby discouraging them from imagining alternative pathways toward potentially greater degrees of democracy (Atkinson 1999).

Given that collaboration enabled foundations to continue to monopolize their core insider status within philanthropy at a time when it had become fashionable for funders to attempt to make that status more inclusive, it is no wonder that the collaboration model became pervasive throughout philanthropy in the 1980s and 1990s. This was a period in which foundations began filling a vacuum left by the federal government amidst its divestment of responsibility for antipoverty reform. Sponsoring collaborations was a way for foundations to maintain their core institutional identity at a time when their policy roles were undergoing transformation. For most of the twentieth century, foundations' role was to seed reforms that, if successful, would spawn into larger federal initiatives. This was the case with the antipoverty demonstration projects funded by the Ford Foundation during the early 1960s and the subsequent war on poverty. Thus, whereas historically foundations had forged collaborations with the federal government, comprehensive community initiatives enabled them to continue collaborating on antipoverty reforms but with a new partner: community-based organizations.

Given that within the political context in which comprehensive community initiatives came about there was strong emphasis placed on private and local solutions to social problems, forging collaboration with community-based organizations legitimized foundations' new policy roles. After all, foundations were private and many community-based organizations worked at the most local level: the neighborhood. Moreover, foundations were purportedly apolitical entities that, unlike government, were ostensibly not bent toward partisanship and reinforcing hierarchy but, quite to the contrary, toward invoking a core American value: the idea that poor people could make significant strides toward improving their lives by participating in the process of antipoverty reform.

The reality, however, was that comprehensive community initiatives became more of a forum for showcasing collaboration as a popular and politically palatable strategy for creating antipoverty reforms than a meaningful vehicle for poor constituencies to exercise influence within these reforms. It is unclear how effectively these initiatives empowered poor people, let alone whether they made a measurable difference in revitalizing low-income neighborhoods or mitigating poverty.

Chapter Seven
Philanthropy and the Media Spotlight

Although the story of the Chicago Initiative was idiosyncratic to a particular time and place, there are two facets of this story that recur when we compare it with other examples of philanthropic responses to media-framed crises. The first is that charitable giving massively increases in the wake of such a crisis, stemming from escalating public concern over the crisis and what can be done to alleviate it. And second, this comparison reveals that significant charitable concern about a particular problem is typically predicated on that problem's capturing and retaining the media spotlight.

COMPARING THE PHILANTHROPIC RESPONSES TO THE 1992 LA RIOTS AND THE 2004 INDIAN OCEAN TSUNAMI

Consider the parallels between the Chicago Initiative and the outpouring of philanthropy following the Indian Ocean tsunami that occurred on December 26, 2004, which devastated the lives of millions of people. The details of these two examples are quite different: riots in Los Angeles versus a natural disaster covering a major portion of the globe; charitable concern by a small cluster of Chicago-area foundations versus a historically unprecedented magnitude of funds, totaling in the billions of dollars, pooled together across international borders. Yet, if we peer for a moment at the forest through the trees, we can see that in both cases the crisis was not only about human suffering, but reflected the fact that these particular stories of suffering had become headline news stories.

In the spring of 1992, millions of Americans watched the dramatic nightly news coverage of the LA riots, often seeing riot footage juxtaposed against replayed airings of the Rodney King beating, which had become a media spectacle in its own right some fourteen months earlier. Similarly, many tourists spending their 2004 Christmas vacation in Thailand, India, or Sri Lanka documented the tsunami on their personal video cameras as it hit the shoreline, and filmed the ensuing scenes of devastation in surrounding coastal areas. These photographed images of horror quickly became the lead news story around the world, and the tsunami became a topic of top concern for ordinary people far and wide.

In making the LA riots and the Indian Ocean tsunami daily headline news over the span of several weeks, media coverage of these two events was similar in that it focused public attention on scenes of grisly devastation and compelled charitable action in response. That the pooling together of millions of dollars in Chicago following the riots and billions of dollars worldwide after the tsunami reflected strong moral intention is certainly not debatable. But, what is interesting about these parallel charitable responses to crisis is that they proved to be contingent upon the crisis being in the media spotlight in the first place.

It is beyond question that the tsunami produced a horror of unfathomable magnitude. Perhaps as many as a quarter of a million people died, and many times that number no longer had adequate food, shelter, and sanitation. But we must also highlight, as United Nations humanitarian chief Jan Egeland publicized soon after the tsunami hit, that more than 30,000 people die every day in the Third World from disasters, like starvation and disease, which receive very little media attention. This means that over any given nine-day period, more people die of preventable causes than were killed by the tsunami (*Boston Globe* 2005). The point of Egeland's raising this comparison was in no way to minimize the magnitude of the tsunami tragedy. His aim was, rather, to inform the world that humanitarian disasters that capture the media spotlight are not necessarily more pressing than those that do not, and indeed those in the spotlight may actually be *less* pressing since they so easily generate charitable contributions.

Viewing the aftermath of the Indian Ocean tsunami as an example of a massive philanthropic response to a media-framed crisis reiterates a core lesson documented by the story of the Chicago Initiative. Due to the sustained media coverage being given to the LA riots, the collaboration was successful in pooling foundation moneys together to fund an expansion of summer opportunities for poor youth. Given the grisly scenes being broadcast from Los Angeles, the possibility that a dearth of such opportunities might be the impetus for violence was a concern very much in the minds of foundation executive directors. But, when it came time to re-frame the goals of the collaboration around neighborhood revitalization—an agenda that was tangential to the media's coverage of the riots—the collaboration lost the buzz that had originally propelled it into action. Moreover, by the time the Initiative's Long-Range Planning Task Force presented funders with a detailed plan for revitalizing poor neighborhoods in Chicago, the LA riots had long ceased being an everyday news story.

In an interview, the executive director of the Chicago Fund compared how, while on the one hand, the news media visually portrayed the LA riots as a crisis demanding immediate philanthropic attention, on the other hand the urban poverty crisis depicted in academic and journalistic writings did not similarly compel such action:

> A riot—you can see it. You could feel it. The moment had happened. You could see the beatings, and the fires, and everything else. And that was very tangible. A book isn't tangible. Some author's description— and we have all kinds of descriptions of issues . . . That's the story of society, I think, to a great degree. As long as it's not in our face, we don't tend to be responsible.

Although whether or not an event can be visually documented is a key factor influencing the extent of news coverage (Bellafante 2005; Firestone 1999), the newness of an event is also critical. Poor neighborhoods that have dilapidated housing and few employment opportunities are certainly not a novel phenomenon, and consequently are not particularly newsworthy. Of course, the same goes for everyday street violence, which is why it was essential that foundations saw the violence in LA as of an entirely different magnitude than the typical kinds of violence that take place in large cities. In this regard, the executive director of Concerned Corporate Citizens commented in an interview:

> That happens every night so that's, you know, what's new? Don't tell me that your summer programs are going to do anything to prevent those crimes that I see on television. No, I'm not going to go to the CEO of some corporation and say, "look, I've got this great summer program. Give us a hundred thousand, or five hundred thousand, and we're going to stop murder, or shootings, or whatever." When I went to them and said, "All the agencies are really worried that this summer, there's going to be a blow-up, not unlike LA, and people are really mad, and hot, and all of that," they understood what I meant. And they said, "Yeah. Here's some money. Let's see if you can at least cool it down a little bit."

PHILANTHROPY AND THE CONSTRUCTION OF SOCIAL PROBLEMS

Although foundations had sincere intentions to act responsibly, their interest in preventing violence following the LA riots was literally a "display" of generosity. Their giving not only piggybacked on the extensive news coverage of the riots but this giving was *predicated,* moreover, on the fact that the problem of urban violence had recently entered the media spotlight. The Chicago Initiative story, alongside the similar and more recent tale concerning charitable responses to the Indian Ocean tsunami, reveals how philanthropy is central to the construction of a problem as an issue of top concern. There is a general social process at work here that explains whether or not a given problem, such as violence in U.S. cities or malnutrition in rural Sri Lanka, becomes an issue of high priority. The powerful role of the news media in initiating this process has been well documented (see Gamson and Modigliani 1989; Johnson 1995; Kerbel 2001). What we learn by looking at the responses to the LA riots and the Indian Ocean tsunami side by side is that philanthropic giving is the next piece of this process, and its role in constructing a social problem is comparably instrumental to that of the news media.

We can think of media coverage of an issue as giving that issue urgency "points." Since there is competition among problems for the attention and concern of those with the resources to address these problems (Loseke 1999), issues that get more coverage are more likely to win the competition. These issues become more familiar to the public as well as to policymakers, and are consequently more inclined to carry a sense of immediacy. Just as news coverage allocates urgency points to some problems over others, giving away charitable money to those issues framed by the media as crises is a way for an individual or a foundation to feel successful at responding in a meaningful way to the seemingly endless abundance of human need. In this regard, the executive director of the Tribunal Foundation made the following comment.

> Every occupation has a system by which, or every field of endeavor has a system by which you score points. And you show you're successful or unsuccessful. In this area you make grants. And the question is: What is the scoring system? And that's exactly what happens in the philanthropic community, is you—how do you know if you're better than the guy down the block as a foundation? You've got to, you take this complex society and you find your niche, and if somebody bigger on the block goes into that niche, then that downgrades you in terms of your

distinctive role and you've got to find a new niche that isn't being over-shadowed by somebody else doing the exact same thing.

Comparing different examples of philanthropic responses to media-framed crises underscores the sociological wisdom that social problems never speak for themselves. Rather, problems must be defined as in need of fixing for them to get societal attention. And some social problems are assigned more urgency than others (Spector and Kitsuse 1987). The preceding discussion suggests that after the news media do the work of spotlighting certain problems, the actions of those who offer their charitable support to address these problems become an additional source of claims-making. Since news coverage frames how people think about the urgency of addressing one problem versus another, philanthropic giving that is concentrated toward issues highlighted by the media serves as a secondary spotlight for these issues.

CONSEQUENCES OF SPOTLIGHTING SOME CRISES OVER OTHERS

The consequences of this tendency for philanthropic giving to go dispro-portionately to issues that capture the media spotlight are significant. Such giving focuses the urgency for problem solving only on certain crises, which threatens to crowd out discussion of other problems simultaneously taking place that may deserve an even greater philanthropic response. This is not only an indication that dollars do not necessarily target the greatest objective human needs but also reveals that certain problems inevitably lose out in the competition for scarce philanthropic resources simply because these problems cannot be readily packaged as feature news stories.

Another important consequence of the tendency for charitable giving to piggyback on media-framed crises is that such giving can leave recipients feeling disillusioned, and even at times resentful. While recipients are ini-tially likely to feel gratitude for being the beneficiary of others' munificence at a time of such grave need, all too often such gratitude becomes tempered by feelings of betrayal because funding promises made while a problem is prominent in the news go unrealized once coverage of the problem recedes.

Such has been the case for people in Honduras whose lives were shat-tered by Hurricane Mitch six years prior to the Indian Ocean tsunami. A couple of weeks after the tsunami, and amidst the blitz of news coverage surrounding it, the *New York Times* ran a story about the current mood among Hondurans whose lives were upended by the Hurricane. The *Times* article initiated recounted that:

> Six years ago it was scenes from Honduras that filled television news-
> casts and newspaper pages. Then as now, there was a public outpour-
> ing of sympathy and support. Then as now, heads of state pledged huge
> amounts of aid. International relief agencies committed themselves to
> "build back better," promising to stay for the long term and provide
> the tools needed to overcome the social and economic forces that make
> the poor so vulnerable (Thompson and Fathi 2005: A1).

Although approximately $9 billion was pledged from around the world,
most of that money was never actually donated. This left people feeling
betrayed, abandoned, and wishing that the TV cameras would return to the
scene of destruction to document how little had changed since the hurricane took place (Thompson and Fathi 2005).

In the parallel case of the Chicago Initiative, many community leaders
were certainly grateful that their organizations got the opportunity to
obtain new sources of grant money for youth programs during the summers of 1992 and 1993. However, disillusionment set in as it became
apparent that the fanfare that foundations had espoused over creating a
long-term collaboration to revitalize poor neighborhoods was mostly just
talk. A black activist who had been working in Chicago since his involvement in the civil rights movement said in an interview:

> I've been around a long time doing this kind of work. Whenever there
> is an upheaval of a major significance, there is a response, and I call it a
> "knee-jerk" response, to that by the private sector to quiet the waters.
> But, once the heat from the incident is over, then we go back to busi-
> ness as usual. And this proved to be true to form [with the Chicago Ini-
> tiative]. No different from what I've seen during the upheavals of the
> 60s and early 70s when we've had major gang upheavals. It becomes
> the "sexy" thing to do. This is the "right" thing to do. Companies allo-
> cate $100,000 to do this, to get as their share, but have no intentions of
> doing it over the long term.

While the reasons for community disillusionment over the Chicago
Initiative may not have been new—unrealized promises of long-term funding for antipoverty reform—the extent of this disillusionment was probably
greater than it had been previously. The rhetoric of collaboration powerfully
invoked a sense of hope among many of the community leaders that participated in the Chicago Initiative that *this time* the funding commitments
would be sustained because the work would be shared collaboratively. Yet,

as we have seen, the Chicago Initiative ended up repackaging old wine in new bottles, and not just in terms of the limited degree of inclusiveness that the collaboration fostered. The collaboration rhetoric also masked the enduring and unchanged reality that the philanthropic framing of the crisis afflicting poor neighborhoods would piggyback on the media framing rather than be transformative. One of the community activists I interviewed summed up the cynicism shared by many of his peers in indicating what a transformative framing of the crisis afflicting poor neighborhoods might include:

> People in communities where there is reported to be an unofficial unemployment rate in excess of sixty percent wonder what more it takes to say "crisis" to a city in terms of the use of its resources. Or when it is just blatantly obvious to everyone in the city that capital funds are not spent in areas where poor people live. And this is not true just for last year; it's a pattern of behavior in this city. And so there are many in the neighborhoods saying "this crisis is here. These are conditions—you know, the sixty- percent dropout rate, the seventy- percent unemployment rate, the drugs and gang warfare. These are critical issues that we are in a state of crisis. Why do we need to spend $2 million because we think LA might happen? It is happening now." That was the point of view of a lot of people in this city.

Community resentment over the Chicago Initiative was, therefore, grounded in the fact that, despite all the fanfare, the Initiative proved to be mostly business as usual. In this vein, a community activist who was part of the Initiative's Long-Range Planning Task Force commented in an interview:

> All the funders want to be stars, and [the executive director of the Chicago Community Trust] had starred with [the summer piece of] the Chicago Initiative. But, stardom only lasts a very short time unless you have a new movie. We didn't have a new movie, and we couldn't create a new movie.

The news media had produced a hit new drama in covering the LA riots, and Chicago foundations proceeded to stake out starring roles in this drama. From the perspective of many community leaders, this was what the Chicago Initiative was ultimately all about, seeding reasons for them to feel disillusioned, resentful, and betrayed yet again by policy elites.

Afterword
The Future of Philanthropic Collaboration

Two trends currently taking place are likely to have profound implications for the future of philanthropic collaboration. First, over the next several decades, as members of the Baby Boom generation die in greater and greater numbers, an unprecedented transfer of wealth will occur. A study published by the Boston College Social Welfare Research Institute in 1999 conservatively estimated that between 1998 and 2052 this wealth transfer will total at least $41 trillion, and may well be double or even triple that amount (Havens and Schervish 1999).

The second trend is that a growing number of successful entrepreneurs are creating foundations that stipulate as a core goal to forge sustained collaborative relationships with grantee organizations. The benefactors of these foundations view collaborating with grantees *not* as a one-time short-term scenario only initiated during special situations of crisis and then abandoned soon afterwards, but rather as a new philanthropic practice. These entrepreneurs outwardly reject the traditional norm of keeping grant recipients at arms length separate and unequal, seeking instead to foster engagement and greater equity between funder and grantee (Frumkin 2000).

These trends jointly indicate that in the coming decades there is likely to be explosive growth in the creation of new foundations, and that collaboration between funders and grantees may well become an institutionalized feature of American philanthropy. But, what will this mean in terms of leveling power imbalances, which collaborations purport to do yet have had only mixed success in achieving to date? Will the Chicago Initiative's story about the gulf between rhetoric and practice simply be replicated in the future? This story conveys some lessons about power sharing that, if heeded, may offer prospects for foundations to do a better job in living up to the promise of collaboration.

Foundations need to change the basic terms upon which they are willing to share power with community-based organizations. Although comprehensive community initiatives set up an unprecedented context for democtraic philanthropy, they were ultimately a paradox in that they imposed implicit limits on community-based organizations' capacity to contribute equally to the partnership. Collaborations must create contexts for power sharing that do not have pre-defined limits. In other words, the power sharing must go beyond the short term, and therefore the largely symbolic. The Chicago Initiative did not, by and large, do this because it did not call into question the basic, institutionalized terms upon which foundations allocate grants.

For foundations, becoming more open to sharing power with community-based organizations does *not* mean renouncing all influence over grantmaking. Indeed, it would be a mistake to derive from the Chicago Initiative story the notion that this initiative would have been more successful if only sponsors had capitulated to community-based organizations since these organizations always best represent the interests of the poor. The point, rather, is that foundations need to make themselves amenable to embracing "partnership" in the fullest sense of the word, which entails mutual decision making between foundations and community-based organizations. This involves considerable give and take between collaborators and a balancing of interests.

Appendix A
The Challenges and Rewards of Undertaking this Study

I began collecting data about the Chicago Initiative in October 1995 and completed my research in February 1997. First, I did a few pilot interviews of some of the Initiative's key players in order to gain a basic familiarity with the collaboration. Next, I combed through the Initiative's documentary history, which is archived at the Chicago Historical Society. This investigative task was cumbersome because, at the time of my research, which was just a few months after the Chicago Initiative had given over its files, these files had not yet been systematically organized by archivists.

Despite this difficulty, I still quickly found out that these historical materials contained a rich array of pertinent information about the day-to-day operation of the Chicago Initiative. I drew data principally from the minutes of meetings of various committees and task forces, and to a lesser extent from memoranda, fundraising and grantmaking statistics, and bound reports.

In May 1996, I began to interview key people who had been involved in the Initiative. In all, I spoke with 60 of the collaboration's leading figures. Since no one person was involved in all aspects of the collaboration, I compiled this sample with the goal of obtaining a representative range of input from individuals working across the collaboration. In attempting to locate informants, the fact that I already had a measure of credibility and legitimacy for what I was undertaking helped me enormously. Two of the leading figures in the Chicago Initiative—a funder and the director of an umbrella organization of grantees—co-signed a letter asking prospective informants that they agree to speak to me. I attached this letter to my written requests for interviews. In my own letter, contained in Table 9, I indicated who I was, what I wanted to find out, and the key fact that I was *not* working for any of the organizations involved in the Initiative. Without a doubt, the authoritative backing that I had from the outset of my research greatly facilitated my data collection. With a simple follow-up phone call a week or so later, most people happily honored my request for an interview.

Still, some people refused to speak to me. Although I took on the project with an institutional stamp of approval, nobody stood to incur major costs by refusing to be interviewed. Indeed, two funders told me pointblank that being interviewed by me was just not worth their time. One community leader never bothered to return my phone calls. I finally gave up after leaving seven messages.

TABLE 9: Letter Requesting Interview

Dear _____:

I am writing in reference to your association with the Chicago Initiative (TCI). At its final meeting before disbanding, there was a consensus within TCI to find someone to do an in-depth analysis of the Initiative's history. Since I am the person undertaking this task, I would very much like to meet with you to discuss your role in TCI and the larger issues that philanthropic collaboration raises.

The interview lasts approximately one hour. My questions are designed to enable you to reflect in an informal way about these issues. Everything we discuss will remain strictly confidential and your identity will be kept anonymous.

I do *not* represent any of the organizations involved in TCI, but am rather a doctoral candidate in sociology at Northwestern University. The enclosed letter from the executive director of United Funders and the executive director of the Chicago Neighborhood Alliance testifies to my credentials and to my research agenda. My basic objective is to understand more about donor-grantee relationships and to assess how differences between these groups affect their possibilities for collaboration.

I would like to conduct this interview at a time that is most convenient for you between the Thanksgiving and Christmas holidays. Should you not be available during this period, then I would be happy to schedule an appointment after the new year. If you have any questions about this research or want to schedule a time to get together, please feel free to call me at (847) 869–7962. Otherwise, I will contact you within the next week. Thank you very much for your time and consideration.

Sincerely,
Ira Silver

My being a well-educated, relatively articulate white male contributed to the fact that, on the whole, funders appeared more comfortable speaking openly to me than were grantees. Since all but three funders were white and most were solidly middle class, they were people with whom I shared sufficient cultural capital to enable the interviews to proceed smoothly, and some of the interviews even contained a considerable measure of rapport. In contrast, most community leaders were people of color and of lower class background, and my interviews with them tended to be more formal. This formality probably had to do with the fact that community leaders were generally suspicious of funders' motives for mobilizing the Chicago Initiative in the first place. As a result, community leaders either may have not wanted to speak with me in depth or may have viewed me as aligned with funders. Thus, my data were inevitably limited by what people chose to share with me. And what they were willing to share was influenced, in ways that I cannot precisely be sure of, by how they perceived me and my connection to the Chicago Initiative.

I still managed to accumulate a wealth of provocative data. I was able to get unparalleled access to two quite distinct social worlds and to capture how these social worlds intersected. Even though some community leaders may have been suspicious of who I was, whose interests I represented, and what I would subsequently do with the data, the majority of them agreed to be interviewed and spoke in depth about the range of topics I raised. This is noteworthy given that very little prior philanthropic research has tapped the social world of grantees, let alone has captured in-depth insight into this social world.[1]

In total, I collected over 2000 pages of interview and archival data. Of course, my research would have been significantly more thorough had I learned about the Chicago Initiative three years earlier and done a participant-observation study of it. I would not only have gained a richer picture of its day-to-day events, but I would have been able to substantiate and confirm the retrospective data that I did collect. In this regard, my data are limited by the fact that they pertain to what people recalled having said and done a few years earlier (via interviews) as well as what one person recorded as the progression of a particular meeting (via meeting minutes), rather than to what actually happened at the time these events were unfolding. This would be a big shortcoming if my data pointed to consensus among actors where it may not have actually existed. While this possibility exists in theory—given that retrospective accounts can easily mask disputes and dissension that actually took place—the reality of my data proved quite different. As the book illustrates, my data consistently point to a variety of political divisions within the Chicago Initiative collaboration. Indeed, these divisions—particularly the ones between funders and grantees—ended up being central to the book as a whole.

Appendix B

Key Dates in the History of the Chicago Initiative

1992

<u>April</u>

29   Four white Los Angeles police officers are acquitted on charges of excessively beating black motorist, Rodney King. Riots break out shortly after the verdict is announced.

<u>May</u>

4   The executive director of the Chicago Fund attends a fundraiser where a friend asks him what the foundation plans to do to keep Chicago "cool" during the upcoming summer.

8   President Bush pledges to a group of community leaders in Los Angeles that Congress would quickly consider a proposal to systematically address poverty in the city.

11   First meeting of the group that subsequently became the Chicago Initiative.

26   Mayor Daley asks the Chicago Park District "to develop some thing for the many children living in the State Street developments." The Park District's proposal was, however, not funded by the Initiative.

      First explicit mention made by funders about the potential long-term implications of the Chicago Initiative.

29   Jobs/Job Training Task Force members testify before U.S. House of Representatives Subcommittee on Human Resources, Committee on Ways and Means.

June

1   Official kickoff meeting of the Chicago Initiative.

12   Grantmaking letter sent out by Businesses for the City and United Funders. Both letters refer to the possible long-term sustainability of the Initiative.

19   Chicago schools close for the summer.

21   Chicago Bulls win their second consecutive National Basketball Association championship. Violence breaks out on the city's West Side.

29   Dated award letter indicating that on June 11th the board of Madison Trust approved a $250,000 grant for "long-term planning activities." This check was returned, eventually to be re-allocated in a $50,000 increment on November 12, 1992 and in a $200,000 allotment on July 12, 1993.

September

22   At a Distribution Committee meeting, the chair of the Long-Range Planning Task Force outlines the findings of the task force's separate working groups on economic development, community development, and family development.

October

13   Seven year-old Dantrell Davis is killed by gang gunfire outside his home in the Cabrini-Green public housing development while on his way to school.

29   Long-Range Planning Task Force issues a working draft of its report entitled "Chicago, Where Communities Work."

November

17   First Meeting of the Committee on the 1993 Summer Grantmaking Campaign.

December

17   Jobs/Job Training Task Force members testify before the Senate Labor and Human Resources Committee, Subcommittee on Employment and Productivity.

18   Long-Range Planning Task Force Report issued.

1993

March

28–30   Visit to the Atlanta Project.

April

--   Madison Trust launches the Collaboration Project.

12   The Chicago Fund sends out invitations to elicit community participation in a second summer grantmaking campaign.

May

3   Official kickoff meeting for the 1993 summer grantmaking campaign.

     President Clinton announces Empowerment Zone/Enterprise Communities legislation.

10–13   Five technical assistance sessions are given for prospective summer grant applicants.

13   Mayor Daley forms a citywide Youth Development Task Force.

June

1   Summer grant proposals due.

16   First meeting of the Mayor's Youth Development Task Force.

18, 24   Summer grants made by Distribution Committee.

24–30   Community conversations are held in preparation for the implementation of the Initiative's neighborhood revitalization agenda.

July

26   Conference on the Future of the American Workplace held in downtown Chicago at Roosevelt University. Mayor Daley and President Clinton each praise the Chicago Laboratory for Change.

August

--   Linked development request for proposals goes out to over 800 individuals and organizations throughout the city.

September

24   Deadline for submitting letter of intent for linked development grants.

October

--   The Chicago Fund agrees to underwrite the costs of the Initiative's strategic planning process.

--   Chicago Lab delegation goes to Washington. Representative Mel Reynolds and Senator Carol Moseley-Braun agree to introduce waivers' legislation into Congress.

November

5   First Strategic Planning Committee Meeting.

8   The Chicago Fund mentions the possibility of an endowment for the Initiative.

December

--   Strategic Planning Committee discusses three possible future scenarios for the Chicago Initiative.

22   Deadline for submitting full proposals for linked development grants. This was requested of 12 of the 64 organizations that sent letters of intent, 25 of which had been given site visits.

1994

January

24   The Distribution Committee awards seven linked development grants.

27   Steering Committee approves Strategic Plan, which recommends that the Initiative continue to operate and adopt a long-range mission for addressing persistent poverty in low-income Chicago communities.

February

--   Strategic Planning Process completed.

March

--   An effort is made to elicit Mayor Daley's renewed participation in the Initiative.

14   Madison Trust's Collaboration Project ends.

April

--   The technical assistance part of the community-building piece begins.

12   Proposed mission statement devised. It focuses on community building, youth development, and policy advocacy.

June

9   Announcement of YouthWorks, the Mayor's Youth Development Task Force recommendation.

September

--   The Chicago Fund announces its intention to scale back its commitment to the Initiative, while still remaining a collaborative partner.

22   First meeting of the Initiative's Youth Development Task Force.

October

4   Chicago Lab begins preparation of a document to be shared with the Department of Health and Human Services regarding what the Lab proposes to do.

December

21   Chicago is designated as 1 of 6 cities for Empowerment Zone funding.

1995

January

--   The Chicago Fund announces that it will designate a representative to the Initiative's Steering Committee and remain its fiscal agent.

March

9   Long-Range Planning Task Force begins to design a grantmaking process for the seven collaborations seeking renewals of funding.

May

31   Dated letter from Madison Trust awarding a two-year $200,000 grant "to support community-building activities and related administrative costs."

June

30   The Chicago Fund terminates its role as the Initiative's fiscal agent.

July

27   Final Steering Committee meeting.

August

31   The Chicago Initiative closes.

Notes

NOTES TO CHAPTER ONE

1. Some commentators refer to these events as the *LA rebellion* rather than the *LA riots*. This distinction is not merely semantic but rather carries an important political message concerning how people viewed the violence in Los Angeles and the factors that triggered it. The basis for this distinction will become clearer in Chapter Four.

2. All of the Chicago Initiative's sponsors were foundations. I use the terms *foundation, sponsor,* and *funder* interchangeably throughout the book. Also, I refer to community-based organizations interchangeably as *grantees.* Even though some of these organizations did not actually receive money from the Chicago Initiative, all of them were prospective grant recipients.

3. These umbrella organizations were groups comprised of either a cluster of funders or a cluster of grantees, and did advocacy work on behalf of these respective groups' interests.

4. This category combines the "Funder" and "Funder Umbrella Organization" categories from Table 1.

5. This category combines the "Grantee" and "Grantee Umbrella Organization" categories from Table 1.

6. This category combines the "City Agency," "Chicago Initiative Staff," and "Other" categories from Table 1.

7. Former Major League Baseball commissioner and 1984 Summer Olympics chairman Peter Ueberroth spearheaded Rebuild LA, a collaboration comprised of leaders from the city government, local businesses, and community-based organizations whose principal goal was to revitalize areas of Los Angeles devastated by the riots (Sterngold 1997).

8. Even though some comprehensive community initiatives are still in operation, since the one I am focusing on in this book is not, I will refer to them as a whole in the past tense.

9. The exception to this trend is the grants given away by "alternative" foundations like the sixteen that comprise the Funding Exchange network.

These foundations support grassroots organizations working for progressive social changes among politically marginalized groups. The motto among these foundations—"change not charity"—reflects a commitment to support organizations working to dismantle the underlying structures of social inequality in the U.S—organizations that often face great obstacles to obtaining support from mainstream foundations because their agendas are simply too radical for these foundations (Ostrander 1995).

NOTES TO CHAPTER TWO

1. The appeal and persuasiveness of this rhetoric proved to matter decidedly more to voters than did its actual veracity. Indeed, during his first term in office, Richard Nixon actually spent *more* on antipoverty programs than did either of his more liberal predecessors in the Oval Office (Lemann 1981).

2. This rhetoric overshadowed the fact that private philanthropy actually comprised less than five percent of the $40 billion that the Reagan administration cut in federal aid to social services and community development. Economic studies done at the time that these cuts were being made, as well as others done more recently, indicate that for every dollar of reduced federal social spending, private giving increases on average by just a few cents. Such evidence did not, however, diminish the Reagan and Bush administrations' cases for cutting social spending. To the contrary, both administrations legitimized these cuts by claiming that because the private sector was more efficient than the public sector in its use of resources, significantly less private money was needed for successful reform than the voluminous amounts wastefully spent by the federal government during the 1960s (Brown 1999; Karl and Karl 1999; Nielsen 1985; Ostrower 1995; Wolpert 1997).

NOTES TO CHAPTER THREE

1. However, we must bear in mind that not all of the turbulence of the sixties was racial. In addition to the pervasive image of black youth rioting in Chicago and many other U.S. cities, there were also many violent protests against the Vietnam War. These protests, which perhaps left no image as lasting as the "Battle of Chicago" at the 1968 Democratic Convention, almost entirely involved agitated whites. For this very reason, these protests probably remained separated in the minds of the funders of the Chicago Initiative from the fears that the black violence of the 1960s had graphically instilled in them (Masotti et al. 1969).

2. Sociological research has insightfully documented that fear is not merely a psychological condition in people's heads that objectively reflects negative events in the world, but is often itself manufactured through the rhetoric and actions of powerful institutions such as corporations, the government, and the news media. Fear-provoking stories carry entertainment value for

audiences and consequently generate power and profits for those propagating these stories (Altheide 2002, Glassner 1999).

3. *Corporate* refers to direct giving by a company or by a company's foundation. *Independent* refers to foundations endowed by a wealthy benefactor that are legally required to allocate grants without direct influence from the donor or the donor's family (Samuels 1997).

4. Rhetoric about the purported value of collaborating across sectors is not limited to philanthropy but rather predominates throughout the business and government sectors as well (see Googins and Rochlin 2000).

5. The distinction drawn here between the manifest and latent functions of funders' actions is the difference between what funders explicitly said were their reasons for supporting the Chicago Initiative and the organizational benefits of sponsorship that went unsaid (see Merton 1967).

NOTES TO CHAPTER FIVE

1. This was not merely fear-mongering rhetoric, for indeed Rosenfeld (1997) argues that the riot was at least partially a reaction to the televised dramatization of the mayhem in Los Angeles that had taken place several weeks earlier.

2. The fundraising hurdle that the Chicago Initiative faced in 1993 is a common one. Consider the similar story of "A Better Chance" during the early 1970s. This program was conceived during the mid 1960s as a means of giving poor children access to elite boarding schools, and it subsequently received massive government and private funding. However, by the early 1970s funders no longer saw this program as new, fresh, and carrying a sense of urgency, and had consequently shifted their priorities elsewhere (Zweigenhaft and Domhoff 1997).

NOTES TO CHAPTER SIX

1. The rhetoric and practices associated with collaboration constitute just one of several ways that elites euphemize the power they exercise within antipoverty policy. See Schram (1995) for a discussion of other examples of policy euphemisms.

2. The focus of this book has been the particularly pronounced impediments to successful collaborations when the partners are foundations and community-based organizations. These impediments, as we have seen, are chiefly the fact that the latter seeks funds from the former coupled with the fact that there are typically vast class and racial barriers between the two groups. Similar impediments also stand in the way of successful collaboration among grantee organizations, which are much more common than funder-grantee collaboration (Kitzi 1997). In addition to class and racial differences that can complicate these collaborations, there are also often ideological and pragmatic differences as well. Indeed, there is as much disjuncture between the rhetoric and reality of collaboration among

grantees as there is between the rhetoric and reality of collaboration between funders and grantees (Ostrower 2005).

NOTES TO APPENDIX A

1. The exception to this dearth of knowledge is the small amount of research that has been done about "alternative" foundations, such as the 16 that comprise the Funding Exchange network. These foundations not only give grants to community-based organizations working for progressive social changes but also empower representatives from these organizations to make grant decisions. Since grantees are so instrumental to how these foundations operate, the various studies that have been done about their grantmaking have also, by extension, offered a window into the social worlds of the grantees themselves (see Odendahl 1990; Ostrander 1995; Ostrander, Silver, and McCarthy 2005; Roelofs 2003; Silver 1997, 1998, forthcoming).

Bibliography

Adler, George. 1994. "Community Action and Maximum Feasible Participation: An Opportunity Lost But Not Forgotten for Expanding Democracy at Home." *Notre Dame Journal of Law, Ethics, and Public Policy* 1994 8(2): 547–71.

Alexander, Jennifer. 1999. "The Impact of Devolution on Nonprofits: A Multiphase Study of Social Service Organizations." *Nonprofit Management and Leadership* 10 (Fall): 57–70.

Altheide, David L. 2002. *Creating Fear: News and the Construction of Crisis.* Hawthorne, NY: Aldine de Gruyter.

Arnove, Robert F. 1980. *Philanthropy and Cultural Imperialism: The Foundations at Home and Abroad.* Bloomington: Indiana University Press.

Atkinson, Rob. 1999. "Discourse of Partnerships and Empowerment in Contemporary British Urban Regeneration." *Urban Studies* 36(1): 59–72.

Baker, Steven, Robert Chaskin, and Joan Wynn. 1996. "The Role of the Sponsor." Pp. 30–35 in *Core Issues in Comprehensive Community-Building Initiatives,* edited by Rebecca Stone. Chicago: Chapin Hall Center for Children, February.

Bellafante, Gina. 2005. "The Power of Images to Create a Cause. " *New York Times,* March 27.

Berman, William C. 1994. *America's Right Turn: From Nixon to Bush.* Baltimore: Johns Hopkins University Press.

Best, Joel. 2003. "The Rhetorical Appeal of Random Violence." Pp. 113–19 in *Social Problems: Constructionist Readings,* edited by Donileen R. Loseke and Joel Best. New York: Aldine de Gruyter.

Bombardieri, Marcella and Walter V. Robinson. 2004. "Wealthiest Nonprofits Favored by Foundations." *Boston Globe,* January 11, 2004. p.1.

Boris, Elizabeth T. 1999. "The Nonprofit Sector in the 1990s." In *Philanthropy and the Nonprofit Sector in a Changing America,* edited by Charles T. Clotfelter and Thomas Ehrlich. Bloomington: Indiana University Press.

Boston Globe. 2005. "Official Fears Drop in Aid for Others" A18.

Bourdieu, Pierre. 1977. *Outline of a Theory of Practice,* translated by Richard Nice. New York: Cambridge University Press.

Boyle, Mary-Ellen, and Ira Silver. 2005. "Poverty, Partnerships, and Privilege: Elite Institutions and Community Empowerment." *City and Community* 4(3): 233–53.

Broderick, Francis L. 1962. "The Fight against Booker T. Washington." Pp. 67–80 in *Booker T. Washington and His Critics: Black Leadership in Crisis*, edited by Hugh Hawkins. Lexington, MA: D.C. Heath.

Brown, Eleanor. 1999. "Patterns and Purposes of Philanthropic Giving." In *Philanthropy and the Nonprofit Sector in a Changing America*, edited by Charles T. Clotfelter and Thomas Ehrlich. Bloomington: Indiana University Press.

Brown, Prudence, Benjamin Butler, and Ralph Hamilton. 2001. *The Sandtown-Winchester Neighborhood Transformation Initiative: Lessons Learned about Community Building & Implementation.* Baltimore: The Annie E. Casey Foundation.

Brown, Prudence and Sunil Garg, 1997. *Foundations and Comprehensive Community Initiatives: The Challenges of Partnership.* Chicago: Chapin Hall Center for Children, April.

Burns, Tom and Gerri Spilka. 1997. *The Planning Phase of the Rebuilding Communities Initiative.* Baltimore: The Annie E. Casey Foundation, July.

Bush, George. 1992. "To Live and Work Together." *Vital Speeches of the Day.* 58(17):514–17.

Chicago Initiative. 1992a. Letter, June 18. Box: Marta White, 1. Folder: Correspondence.

——. 1992b. "The Chicago Initiative: A Plan for Action." Box: 1992, 5. Folder: The Chicago Initiative.

——. 1992c. "Implementation of The Chicago Initiative." Box: 1992, #5. Folder: (Un-named).

——. 1992d. "Jobs/Job Training Task Force: The Chicago Initiative." Box: 1992, 5. Folder: The Chicago Initiative.

——. 1992e. "Number of Jobs Created Per Grant." Box: Marta White #4. Folder: Strategic Planning.

——. 1992f. "Jobs/Job Training Task Force Initial Program Priorities." Box: 1992, #6. Folder: Jobs/Job Training Task Force Initial Program Priorities.

——. 1992g. Letter, July 5. Box: Distribution #1: Folder: (Unnamed).

——. 1992h. Minutes from Emergency Response Coordinating Task Force Meeting, May 27. Box: 1992, 1. Folder: (Un-named).

——. 1992i. "Emergency Response Coordinating Task Force." Box: 1993 Files, 8. Folder: Emergency Response Task Force.

——. 1992j. Memo, June 8. "Media Participation in the Chicago Initiative." Box: 1992, 5. Folder: Chicago Initiative.

——. 1992k. "Report of Funders' Affinity Group Meeting." Box: 1993 Files, #4. Folder: CI Steering Committee Meetings.

——. 1992l. Letter #1, June 12. Box: Marta White, 1. Folder: Correspondence.

——. 1992m. Letter #2, June 12. Box: Marta White, 1. Folder: Correspondence.

——. 1992n. Minutes from Distribution Committee meeting, June 11. Box: 1992, 5. Folder: Chicago Initiative.

——. 1992o. "The Chicago Initiative Long Range Planning Task Force Report." Box: Marta White #1. Folder: Reports.

——. 1992p. Letter, received June 16. Box: 1992, 5. Folder: Chicago Initiative.

——. 1993a. "The Chicago Initiative: A Community Response." Box: Marta Whites Files #1. Folder: Correspondence.

——. 1993b. "Collaborative Ventures Interim Report on the Research Component, October 1993." Box: Marta White #2, Folder: Collaboration Project.

——. 1993c. "Report of the Chicago Initiative Committee on the 1993 Summer Component." Box: Marta White 1. Folder: TCI Funded Projects '92.

——. 1993d. "The Chicago Initiative Highlights." Box: Marta White 1. Folder: TCI Funded Projects '92.

——. 1993e. Chicago Initiative Newsletter, November. Box: Funders' Files 1. Folder: Attachments.

——. 1993f. Memo, April 23. Box: Funders' Files 1. Folder: Attachments.

——. 1993g. Letter, May 13. Box: Marta White 1. Folder: Correspondence.

——. 1993h. "Empowerment Zones." Office of Media Affairs: For Immediate Release. Box: 1993 Files, 2. Folder: To Do.

——. 1993i. Letter, November 10. Box: 1993 Files, 8. Folder: Correspondence Sent.

——. 1993j. "The Chicago Initiative 1993: Communities That Work." Box: Marta White #1. Folder: TCI Funded Projects '92.

——. 1993k. Letter, April 8. Box: Marta White Files #1. Folder: 92/93 Grants Information.

——. 1993l. Letter, April 12. Box: 1993 Files #5. Folder: Requests for Proposals.

——. 1993m. "The Chicago Initiative *Final Progress Report on 1993 Summer Grants.*" Box: Marta White #4. Folder: Strategic Planning.

——. 1993n. Memo, July 28. Box: Administration 3. Folder: Jasculca-Terman and Associates.

——. 1993o. Minutes from Steering Committee meeting, November 8. Box: 1993 Files,7. Folder: Steering Committee.

——. 1993p. Letter, undated. Box: Administration. Folder: RFPs.

——. 1993q. Letter, June 15. Box: Marta White #4. Folder: Strategic Planning.

——. 1993r. Memo, November 3. Box: 1993 Files, 7. Folder: Long Range.

——. 1993s. Letter, undated. Box: 1993 Files, 8. Folder: Correspondence Sent.

——. 1993t. Letter, April 29. Box: Marta White Files #1. Folder: TCI Funded Projects '92, Funders' "Potential" '93.

——. 1993u. Letter, June 2. Box: Funders' Files 1. Folder: Attachments.

——. 1993v. Letter, May 20. Box: Marta White 1. Folder: TCI Funded Projects '92.

——. 1994a. "The Chicago Initiative Proposed Mission Statement." Box: Marta White #4. Folder: Strategic Planning.

——. 1994b. Minutes from Steering Committee meeting, January 27. Box: 1993 Files, 7. Folder: Steering Committee.

——. 1994c. Minutes from Executive Committee meeting, February 11. Box: 1993 Files, 7. Folder: Executive Committee.

——. 1994d. Memo, September 1. Box: 1993 Files, 7. Folder: Youth Development Task Force.

——. 1994e. Memo, May 26. Box: 1993 Files, 7. Folder: Executive Committee.

——. 1994f. "The Chicago Initiative Work Plan: A Discussion Document," June 23. Box: 1993 Files, 7. Folder: Executive Committee Meetings.

——. 1994g. Minutes from Youth Development Task Force Meeting, September 22. Box: 1993Files, 7. Folder: Youth Development Task Force.

——. 1994h. Minutes from Steering Committee Meeting, October 11. Box: 1993 Files, 8. Folder: Steering Committee.

——. 1994i. Minutes from Youth Development Task Force Meeting, December 5. Box: 1993 Files, 7. Folder: Youth Development Task Force.

——. 1994j. "Youth Development Task Force Statement of Purpose for 1995 Funding Cycle." Box: Marta White's Files #1. Folder: Youth Development Task Force.

——. 1994k. Memo, September 9. Box: Marta White #4. Folder: TCI Leadership Committee.

——. 1994l. "Funding Decisions Approved by Distribution Committee, January 1994." Box: 1993 Files, 7. Folder: Long Range.

——. 1994m. Letter, February 10. Box: 1993 Files, 7. Folder: Executive Committee Comments.

——. 1995a. Minutes from Steering Committee meeting, July 27. Box: Marta White #4. Folder: Steering Committee.

——. 1995b. "Overview of Key Decisions for TCI Youth Development Program," February 3. Box: 1993 Files, 7. Folder: Youth Development Task Force.

——. 1995c. Letter, April 25. Box: Marta White #1. Folder: Correspondences.

——. 1995d. Minutes from Youth Development Task Force meeting, April 27. Box: 1993 Files, 7. Folder: Youth Development Task Force.

——. 1995e. Minutes from Steering Committee meeting, January 19. Box: Marta White #4. Folder: Steering Committee.

——. 1995f. Letter, March 28. Box: Funders Files 1. Folder: Attachments.

——. 1995g. Letter, January 19. Box: Funders' Files 2. Folder: Proposals Sent January.

Cloud, Jr., Sanford. 1991. "The Changing Role of Government and its Impact on the Nonprofit and Business Sectors." Pp. 50–59 in *The Corporate Contributions Handbook: Devoting Private Means to Public Needs,* edited by James P. Shannon. San Francisco: Jossey-Bass.

Cloward, Richard A., and Lloyd E. Ohlin. 1960. *Delinquency and Opportunity: A Theory of Delinquent Gangs.* Glencoe, IL: Free Press.

Cohn, Jules. 1970. "Is Business Meeting the Challenge of Urban Affairs?" *Harvard Business Review* 48:68–82.

Colwell, Mary Anna. 1993. *Private Foundations and Public Policy: The Political Role of Philanthropy.* New York: Garland Publishing.

Curti, Merle and R. Nash. *Philanthropy in the Shaping of American Higher Education.* New Brunswick, NJ: Rutgers University Press, 1965.

Daniels, Arlene Kaplan. 1987. *Invisible Careers: Women Civic Leaders from the Volunteer World.* Chicago: University of Chicago Press.

Deakin, Nicholas. 2001. "Public Policy, Social Policy and Voluntary Organisations." Pp. 21–36 in *Voluntary Organisations and Social Policy in Britain,* edited by Margaret Harris and Colin Rochester. New York: Palgrave.

DiMaggio, Paul, and Michael Useem. 1978. "Social Class and Arts Consumption: The Origins and Consequences of Class Differences in Exposure to the Arts in America. *Theory and Society* 5:141–62.

Du Bois, W.E.B. 1962 {1940}. "My Early Relations with Booker T. Washington." Pp. 47–55 in *Booker T. Washington and His Critics: Black Leadership in Crisis,* edited by Hugh Hawkins. Lexington, MA: D.C. Heath.

Edelman, Murray. 1974. "The Political Language of the 'Helping Professions.'" *Politics and Society* 4(3): 295–310.

Farber, David. 1988. *Chicago '68.* Chicago: University of Chicago Press.

Firestone, David. 1999. "One of These Pictures is Worth 1,000 Words." *New York Times,* May 9.

Fisher, Donald. 1983. "The Role of Philanthropic Foundations in the Reproduction and Production of Hegemony." *Sociology* 17: 206–33.

Fishman, Nancy and Meredith Phillips. 1993. *A Review of Comprehensive, Collaborative Persistent Poverty Initiatives.* Evanston, IL: Center for Urban Affairs and Policy Research, June.

Frumkin, Peter. 1999. "Private Foundations as Public Institutions: Regulation, Professionalization, and the Redefinition of Organized Philanthropy." Pp. 69–98 in *Philanthropic Foundations: New Scholarship, New Possibilities,* edited by Ellen Condliffe Lagemann. Bloomington: Indiana University Press, 1999.

——. 2000. "The Face of the New Philanthropy." *The Responsive Community* Summer: 41–48.

Galaskiewicz, Joseph. 1985. *Social Organization of an Urban Grants Economy: A Study of Business Philanthropy and Nonprofit Organizations.* New York: Academic Press.

Gamson, William A., and Andre Modigliani. 1989. "Media Discourse and Public Opinion on Nuclear Power." *American Journal of Sociology* 95(1): 1–37.

Glassner, Barry. 1999. *The Culture of Fear: Why Americans are Afraid of the Wrong Things.* New York: Basic Books.

Gold, Steven. 1997. "Religious Agencies, Immigrant Settlement, and Social Justice." Pp. 47–65 in *Research in Social Policy: Social Justice Philanthropy,* Volume 5, edited by John H. Stanfield, II. Greenwich, CT: JAI Press.

Googins, Bradley K., and Steven A. Rochlin. 2000. "Creating the Partnership Society: Understanding the Rhetoric and Reality of Cross-Sectoral Partnerships." *Business and Society Review* 105(1): 127–44.

Green, Alice P., and Frankie Y. Bailey. 1997. "African Americans in the Private Sector Addressing Crime and the Criminal Justice System." Pp. 67–79 in *Research in Social Policy: Social Justice Philanthropy,* Volume 5, edited by John H. Stanfield, II. Greenwich, CT: JAI Press.

Green, Charles. 1997. "The Black Church in the Struggle for Housing and Neighborhood Revitalization." Pp. 81–96 in *Research in Social Policy: Social Justice Philanthropy,* Volume 5, edited by John H. Stanfield, II. Greenwich, CT: JAI Press.

Haines, Herbert H. 1984. "Black Radicalization and the Funding of Civil Rights: 1957–1970." *Social Problems* 32(1): 31–43.

——. 1988. *Black Radicals and the Civil Rights Mainstream, 1954–1970.* Knoxville: University of Tennessee Press.

Halpern, Robert. 1995. *Rebuilding the Inner City.* New York: Columbia University Press.

Harrington, Michael. 1962. *The Other America: Poverty in the United States*. New York: Macmillan.

Havens, John J., and Paul G. Schervish. 1999. *Millionaires and the Millennium: New Estimates of the Forthcoming Wealth Transfer and the Prospects for a Golden Age of Philanthropy*. Boston College Social Welfare Research Institute.

Himmelstein, Jerome L. 1990. *To the Right: The Transformation of American Conservatism*. Berkeley: University of California Press.

Hubbard, Howard. 1968. "Five Long Hot Summers and How They Grew." *The Public Interest*. 12:3–24.

Hunt, Darnell M. 1997. *Screening the Los Angeles "Riots."* New York: Cambridge University Press.

Jackall, Robert. 1988. *Moral Mazes: The World of Corporate Managers*. New York: Oxford University Press.

Jencks, Christopher. 1987. "Who Gives to What?" Pp. 321–39 in *The Nonprofit Sector: A Research Handbook*, edited by Walter W. Powell. New Haven: Yale University Press.

Jenkins, J. Craig. 1989. "Social Movement Philanthropy and American Democracy." Pp. 292–314 in *Philanthropic Giving: Studies in Varieties and Goals*, edited by Richard Magat. New York: Oxford University Press.

———. 1998. "Channeling Social Protest: Foundation Patronage of Contemporary Social Movements." Pp. 206–16 in *Private Action and the Public Good*, edited by Walter Powell and Elisabeth S. Clemens. New Haven: Yale University Press.

Jenkins, J. Craig, and Craig M. Eckert. 1986. "Channeling Black Insurgency: Elite Patronage and Professional Social Movement Organizations in the Development of the Black Movement." *American Sociological Review* 51:812–29.

Johnson, John M. 1995. "Horror Stories and the Construction of Child Abuse." Pp. 17–32 in *Images of Issues: Typifying Contemporary Social Problems*, Second Edition, edited by Joel Best. Hawthorne, New York: Aldine de Gruyter.

Jones. Peris S. 2003. Urban Regeneration's Poisoned Chalice: Is There an Impasse in (Community) Participation-based Policy? *Urban Studies*. 40(3):581–602.

Karl, Barry D. and Alice W. Karl. 1999. "Foundations and the Government: A Tale of Conflict and Consensus." In *Philanthropy and the Nonprofit Sector in a Changing America*, edited by Charles T. Clotfelter and Thomas Ehrlich. Bloomington: Indiana University Press.

Karl, Barry D., and Stanley N. Katz. 1981. "The American Private Foundation and the Public Sphere 1890–1930." *Minerva* 19:236–70.

———. 1987. "Foundations and Ruling Class Elites." *Daedalus* 116(1):1–40.

Katz, Michael B. 1986. *In the Shadow of the Poorhouse: A Social History of Welfare in America*. New York: Basic Books.

———. 1989. *The Undeserving Poor: From the Poor on Poverty to the War on Welfare*. New York: Pantheon Books.

———. 1995. *Improving Poor People*. Princeton: Princeton University Press.

Kerbel, Matthew R. 2001. *If it Bleeds, it Leeds: An Anatomy of Television News*. Boulder, CO: Westview Press.

Kingdon, John W. 1995. *Agendas, Alternatives, and Public Policies*. New York: HarperCollins College Publishers.

Kirkland, Richard I. 1992. "What Can We Do Now." *Fortune* June 1:41–48.

Kitzi, Jerry. 1997. "Easier Said Than Done." *Foundation News & Commentary* March/April: 39–41.

Kubisch, Anne C. 1996. "Change May Come only at the Price of Charity." Pp. 37–38 in *Core Issues in Comprehensive Community-Building Initiatives*, edited by Rebecca Stone. Chicago: Chapin Hall Center for Children.

Lemann, Nicholas. 1981. *The Promised Land*. New York: Alfred A. Knopf.

Lenkowsky, Leslie. 1999. "Reinventing Philanthropy." In *Philanthropy and the Nonprofit Sector in a Changing America*, edited by Charles T. Clotfelter and Thomas Ehrlich. Bloomington: Indiana University Press.

Loseke, Donileen R. 1997. "'The Whole Spirit of Modern Philanthropy': The Construction of the Idea of Charity, 1912–1992." *Social Problems* 44(4):425–42.

———. 1999. *Thinking about Social Problems: An Introduction to Constructionist Perspectives*. Hawthorne, NY: Aldine de Gruyter.

MacLeod, Jay. 2004. *Ain't No Makin' It: Aspirations and Attainment in a Low-Income Neighborhood*, second edition reissue. Boulder, CO: Westview Press.

Maloney, William A, Grant. Jordan, and Andrew M. McLaughlin. 1994. "Interest Groups and Public Policy: The Insider/Outsider Model Revisited." *Journal of Public Policy* 14(1):17-38.

Masotti, Louis H., Jeffrey K. Hadden, Kenneth F. Seminatore, and Jerome R. Corsi. 1969. *A Time to Burn: An Evaluation of the Present Crisis in Race Relations*. Chicago: Rand-McNally.

Massey, Douglas S., and Nancy A. Denton. 1993. *American Apartheid: Segregation and the Making of the Underclass*. Cambridge: Harvard University Press.

McAdam, Doug. 1982. *Political Process and the Development of Black Insurgency*. Chicago: University of Chicago Press.

McCarthy, John, and Mayer Zald. 1977. "Resource Mobilization and Social Movements." *American Journal of Sociology* 82:1212–41.

Merton, Robert K. 1967. "Manifest and Latent Functions." Pp. 73–138 in *On Theoretical Sociology*. New York: Free Press.

Mills, C. Wright. 1940. "Situated Actions and Vocabularies of Motive." *American Sociological Review* 5(6):904–13.

Morris, Aldon. 1984. *The Origin of the Civil Rights Movement*. New York: Free Press.

Moynihan, Daniel Patrick. 1969. *Maximum Feasible Misunderstanding: Community Action in the War on Poverty*. New York: The Free Press.

Nickerson, Matthew. 1992. "Sniper Kills Cabrini Kid Steps from School." *Chicago Tribune* October 14.

Nielsen, Waldemar A. 1985. *The Golden Donors: A New Anatomy of the Great Foundations*. New York: E.P. Dutton.

Oberschall, Anthony. 1973. *Social Conflicts and Social Movements*. Englewood Cliffs, NJ: Prentice-Hall.

O'Connor, Alice. 1999. "The Ford Foundation and Philanthropic Activism in the 1960s." Pp. 169–94 in *Philanthropic Foundations: New Scholarship, New*

Possibilities, edited by Ellen Condliffe Lagemann. Bloomington: Indiana University Press.

Odendahl, Teresa. 1987. *America's Wealthy and the Future of Foundations*. New York: The Foundation Center.

——. 1990. *Charity Begins at Home: Generosity and Self-Interest among the Philanthropic Elite*. New York: Basic Books.

Ostrander, Susan. 1984. *Women of the Upper Class*. Philadelphia: Temple University Press.

——. 1995. *Money for Change: Social Movement Philanthropy at Haymarket People's Fund*. Philadelphia: Temple University Press.

Ostrander, Susan A., and Paul G. Schervish. 1990. "Giving and Getting: Philanthropy as a Social Relation." Pp. 67–98 in *Issues in American Philanthropy: Strengthening Theory and Practice*, Edited by Jon Van Til and Associates. San Francisco: Jossey-Bass.

Ostrander, Susan A., Ira Silver, and Deborah McCarthy. 2005. "Mobilizing Money Strategically: Grantee Agency, the Funding Dilemma, and Social Change Philanthropy." In *Foundations for Social Change: Critical Perspectives on Philanthropy and Popular Movements*, Edited by Daniel Faber and Deborah McCarthy. New York: Rowman and Littlefield.

Ostrower, Francie. 1995. *Why the Wealthy Give: The Culture of Elite Philanthropy*. Princeton: Princeton University Press.

——. 2005. "The Reality underneath the Buzz of Partnerships: The Potentials and Pitfalls of Partnering." *Stanford Social Innovation Review* Spring: 34–41.

Patterson, James T. 2000. *America's Struggle against Poverty in the Twentieth Century*. Cambridge: Harvard University Press.

Piven, Francis Fox, and Richard Cloward. 1977. *Poor People's Movements*. New York: Pantheon.

Roelofs, Joan. 2003. *Foundations and Public Policy: The Mask of Pluralism*. Albany: State University of New York Press.

Rosenfeld, Michael J. 1997. "Celebrating, Politics, Selective Looting and Riots: A Micro Level Study of the Bulls Riot of 1992 in Chicago." *Social Problems* 44(4):483–502.

Samuels, David G. 1997. "The Regulation of Private Foundations." *New York Law Journal* May 21.

Schram, Sanford E. 1995. *Words of Welfare: The Poverty of Social Science and the Social Science of Poverty*. Minneapolis: University of Minnesota Press.

——. 2000. *After Welfare: The Culture of Postindustrial Social Policy*. New York: New York University Press.

Scott, James C. 1985. *Weapons of the Weak: Everyday Forms of Peasant Resistance*. New Haven: Yale University Press.

——. 1989. "Prestige as the Public Discourse of Domination." *Cultural Critique* 12: 145–66.

——. 1990. *Domination and the Arts of Resistance: Hidden Transcripts*. New Haven: Yale University Press.

Silver, Ira. 1997. "Constructing 'Social Change' Through Philanthropy: Boundary Framing and the Articulation of Vocabularies of Motives for Social Movement Participation." *Sociological Inquiry* 67(4):488–503.

——. 1998. "Buying an Activist Identity: Reproducing Class through Social Movement Philanthropy." *Sociological Perspectives* 41(2):303–21.

——. Forthcoming. "Disentangling Class from Philanthropy: The Double-Edged Sword of Alternative Giving." *Critical Sociology.*

Skocpol, Theda. 2003. *Diminished Democracy: From Membership to Management in American Civic Life.* Norman, OK: University of Oklahoma Press.

Skrentny, John David, 1996. *The Ironies of Affirmative Action: Politics, Culture, and Justice in America.* Chicago: University of Chicago Press.

Smith, James Allen. 1999. "The Evolving American Foundation." In *Philanthropy and the Nonprofit Sector in a Changing America,* edited by Charles T. Clotfelter and Thomas Ehrlich. Bloomington: Indiana University Press.

Spector, Malcolm, and John I. Kitsuse. 1987. *Constructing Social Problems.* New York: Walter de Gruyter.

Stagner, Matthew W, and M. Angela Duran. 1997. "Comprehensive Community Initiatives: Principles, Practice, and Lessons Learned." *Children and Poverty* 7(2):132–40.

Sterngold, James. 1997. "Five Yeas After Los Angeles Riots, Inner City Still Cries out for Jobs." *New York Times* April 28.

Suleiman, Layla. 1994. *Working Toward Citywide Collaboration: Frontline Perspectives on the Chicago Initiative and Recommendations for the Future.* January. Chicago Historical Society, Box: 1993 Files, #7. Folder: Executive Committee, 17.

Taylor, Marilyn. 2001. "Partnerships: Insiders and Outsiders." Pp. 94–107 in *Voluntary Organisations and Social Policy in Britain,* edited by Margaret Harris and Colin Rochester. New York: Palgrave, 2001.

Thompson, Ginger and Nazila Fathi. 2005. "For Honduras and Iran, World's Aid Evaporated." *New York Times.* January 11.

Tilly, Charles. 1978. *From Mobilization to Revolution.* Reading, MA: Addison-Wesley.

Trattner, Walter I. 1984. *From Poor Law to Welfare State: A History of Social Welfare in America,* third edition. New York: The Free Press.

Voices from the Field: Learning from the Early Work of Comprehensive Community Initiatives. 1997. Washington, DC: The Aspen Institute.

Waddan, Alex. 1997. *The Politics of Social Welfare.* Brookfield, VT: Edward Elgar Publishing Company.

Walsh, Joan. 1997. "Community Building in Theory and Practice: Three Case Studies." *National Civic Review* 86(4):291–314.

——. 1999. *The Eye of the Storm: Ten Years on the Front Lines of New Futures.* Baltimore: The Annie E. Casey Foundation.

Washington, Booker T. 1962 [1884]. "The Educational Outlook in the South." Pp. 10–17 in *Booker T. Washington and His Critics: Black Leadership in Crisis,* edited by Hugh Hawkins. Lexington, MA: D.C. Heath.

Weaver, R. Kent. 2000. *Ending Welfare as We Know It*. Washington, DC: Brookings Institution Press.

Willis, Paul. 1977. *Learning to Labor: How Working Class Kids Get Working Class Jobs*. New York: Columbia University Press.

Wolpert, Julian. 1997. "How Federal Cutbacks Affect the Charitable Sector." In *State Devolution in America*, edited by Lynn A. Staeheli, Janet E. Kodras, and Colin Flint. Thousand Oaks, CA: Sage Publications.

Zarefsky, David. 1986. *President Johnson's War on Poverty: Rhetoric and History*. Birmingham: University of Alabama Press.

Zolberg, Vera. 1974. *The Art Institute of Chicago: The Sociology of a Cultural Organization*. Unpublished Doctoral Dissertation. Department of Sociology, University of Chicago.

Zweigenhaft, Richard L., and G. William Domhoff. 1997. "Sophisticated Conservatives and the Integration of Prep Schools: The Creation, Funding, and Evolution of the 'A Better Chance' Program." Pp. 223–40 in *Research in Social Policy: Social Justice Philanthropy*, volume 5, edited by John H. Stanfield II. Greenwich, CT: JAI Press.

Index

9 780415 654678